Rock'N'Roll
for Easy Guitar

This publication is not authorised for sale in
the United States of America and/or Canada

HAL LEONARD EUROPE
Distributed by Music Sales

Exclusive Distributors:
Music Sales Limited
8/9 Frith Street, London W1V 5TZ, England.
Music Sales Pty Limited
120 Rothschild Avenue, Rosebery, NSW 2018, Australia.

Order No. HLE90000540
ISBN 0-7119-7827-1
This book © Copyright 2000 by Hal Leonard Europe.

Unauthorised reproduction of any part of this publication by
any means including photocopying is an infringement of copyright.

Cover design by Hilite Design & Reprographics Limited.
Photography courtesy of London Features International & Redferns.
Printed in the United States of America.

Your Guarantee of Quality:
As publishers, we strive to produce every book to the highest commercial standards.
The book has been carefully designed to minimise awkward page turns and
to make playing from it a real pleasure.
Throughout, the printing and binding have been planned to ensure a
sturdy, attractive publication which should give years of enjoyment.
If your copy fails to meet our high standards, please inform us and we will gladly replace it.

Music Sales' complete catalogue describes thousands of
titles and is available in full colour sections by subject, direct from Music Sales Limited.
Please state your areas of interest and send a cheque/postal order for £1.50 for postage to:
Music Sales Limited, Newmarket Road, Bury St. Edmunds, Suffolk IP33 3YB, England.

www.musicsales.com

All I Have To Do Is Dream The Everly Brothers 4
All Shook Up Elvis Presley 7
At The Hop Danny & The Juniors 9
Blue Suede Shoes Carl Perkins 12
Dizzy Miss Lizzie The Beatles 14
Don't Be Cruel (To A Heart That's True) Elvis Presley 17
Great Balls Of Fire Jerry Lee Lewis 20
Hound Dog Elvis Presley 23
I Want To Hold Your Hand The Beatles 25
Jailhouse Rock Elvis Presley 27
Johnny B. Goode Chuck Berry 29
Long Tall Sally Little Richard 33
Oh, Pretty Woman Roy Orbison 35
Peggy Sue Buddy Holly 40
Rock And Roll Is Here To Stay Danny & The Juniors 42
Rock Around The Clock Bill Haley & His Comets 46
Searchin' The Coasters 48
Shake, Rattle And Roll Bill Haley & His Comets 52
Susie-Q Dale Hawkins 54
That'll Be The Day The Crickets 56
Tutti Frutti Little Richard 59
Wake Up Little Susie The Everly Brothers 61

Strum & Pick Patterns 64

All I Have to Do Is Dream

Words and Music by Boudleaux Bryant

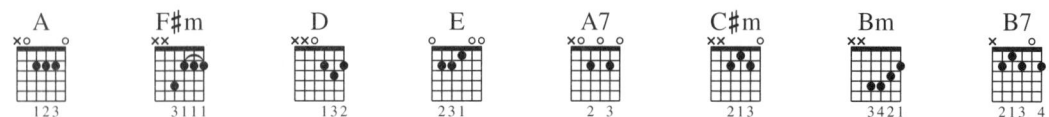

Strum Pattern: 3
Pick Pattern: 3

Dream, _____ dream, dream, dream. _____

Dream, _____ dream, dream, dream. _____ 1. When

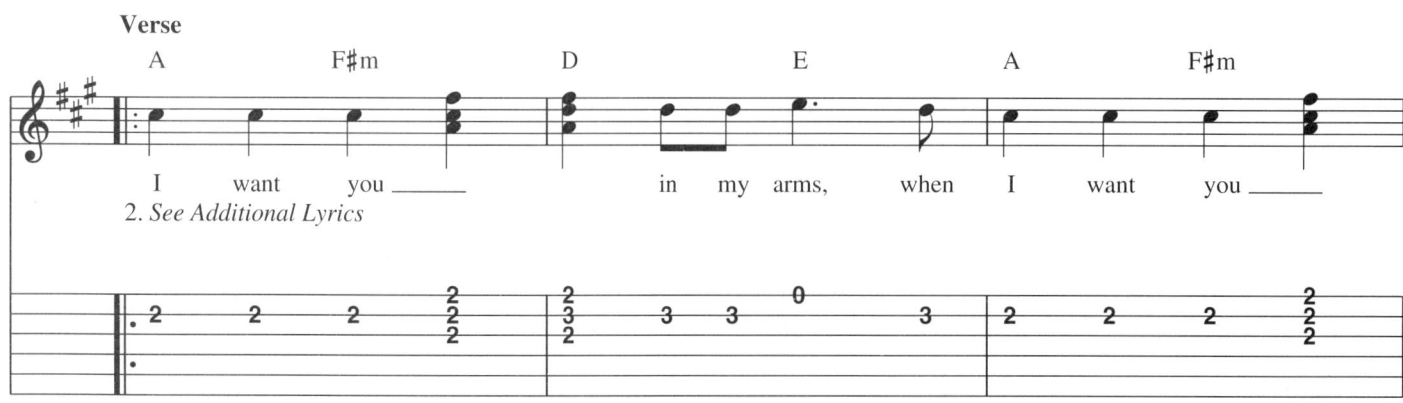

I want you _____ in my arms, when I want you _____

2. See Additional Lyrics

Copyright © 1958 by HOUSE OF BRYANT PUBLICATIONS, Gatlinburg, TN
Copyright Renewed
All Foreign Rights controlled by Acuff-Rose-Opryland Music, Inc., Nashville, TN
International Copyright Secured All Rights Reserved

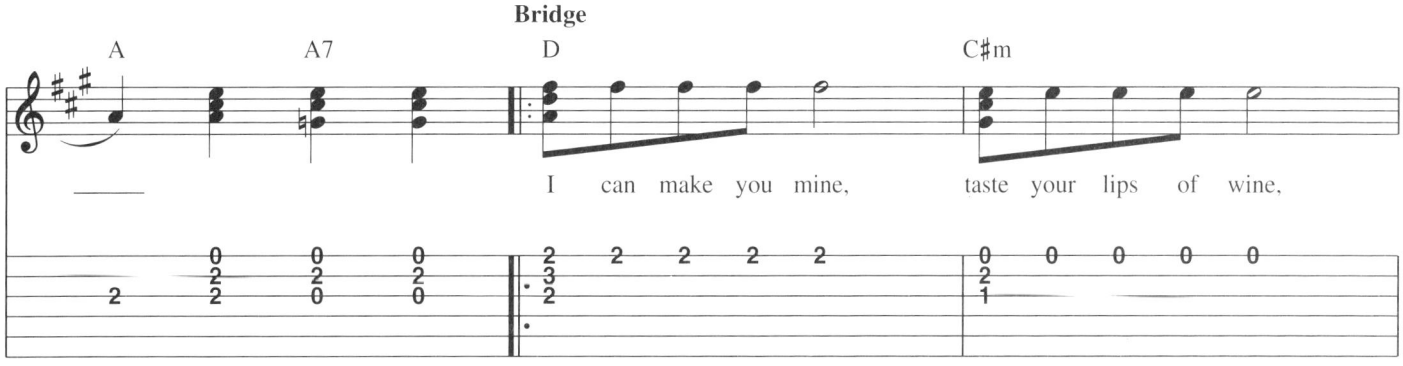
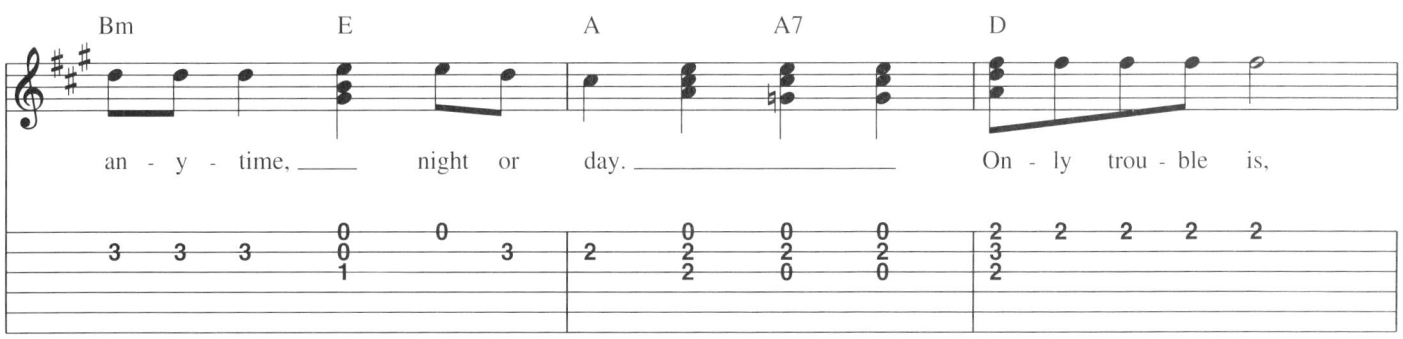

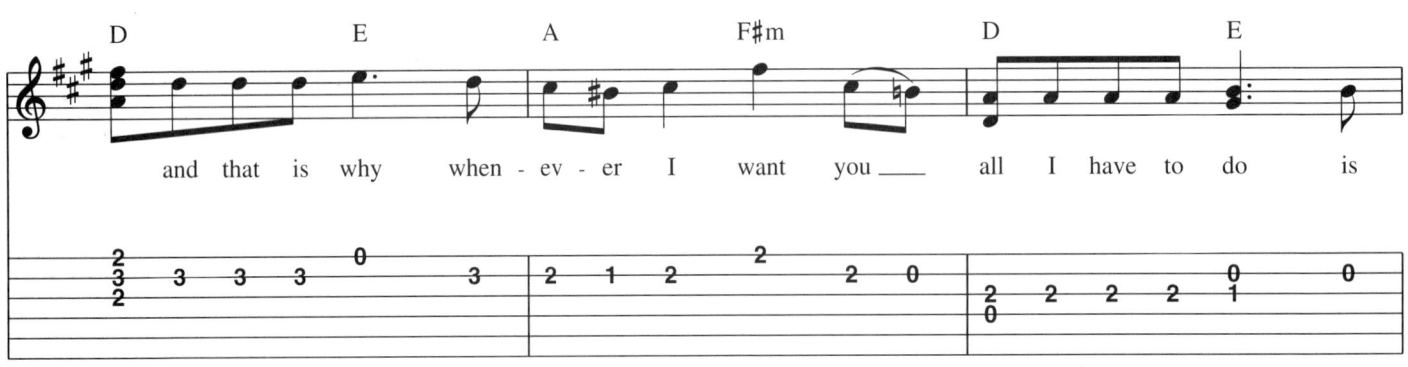
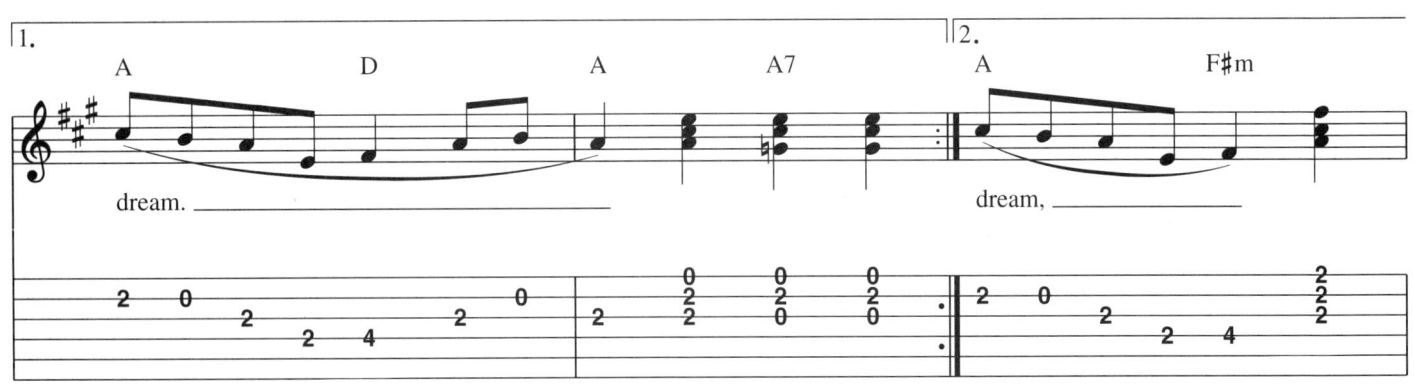
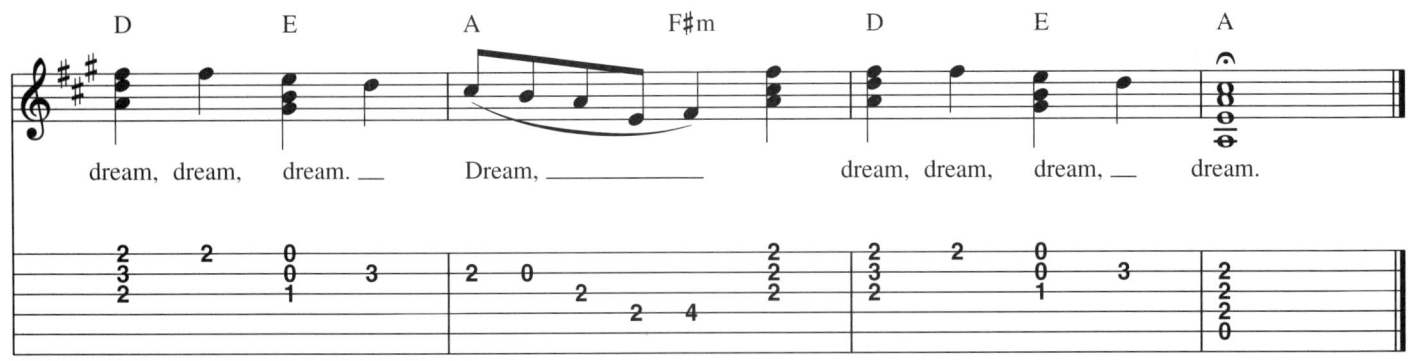

Additional Lyrics

2. When I feel blue in the night,
And I need you to hold me tight,
Whenever I want you
All I have to do is dream.

All Shook Up

Words and Music by Otis Blackwell and Elvis Presley

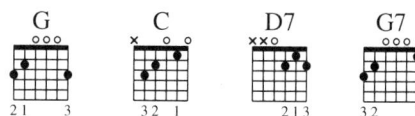

Strum Pattern: 3, 4
Pick Pattern: 3, 5

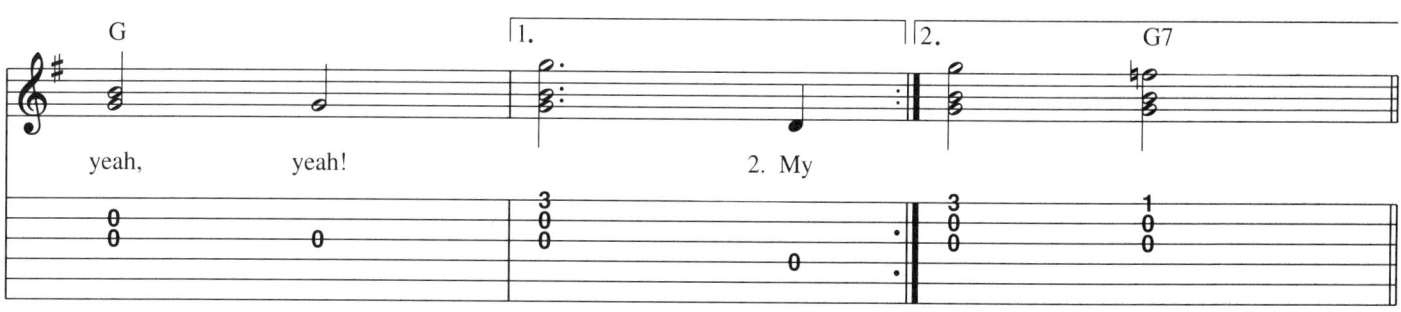

Copyright © 1957 by Shalimar Music Corporation
Copyright Renewed and Assigned to Elvis Presley Music (Administered by R&H Music)
International Copyright Secured   All Rights Reserved

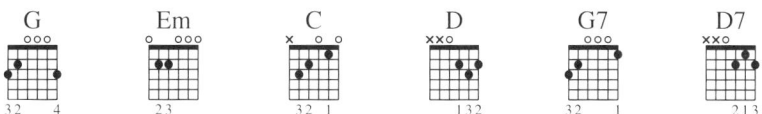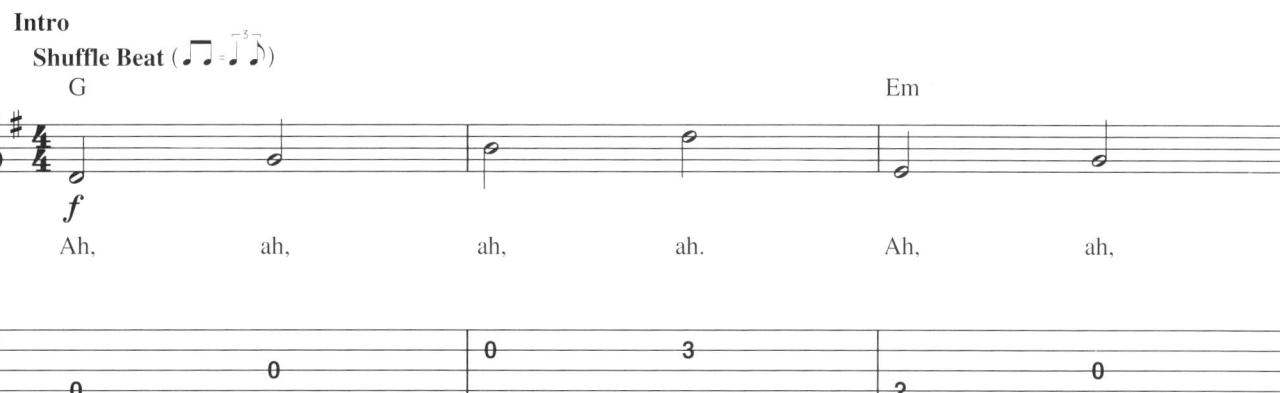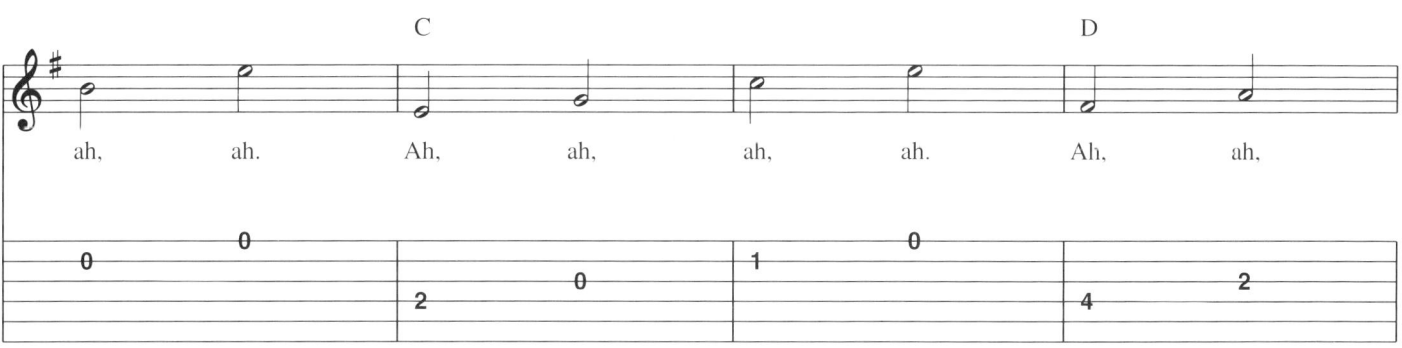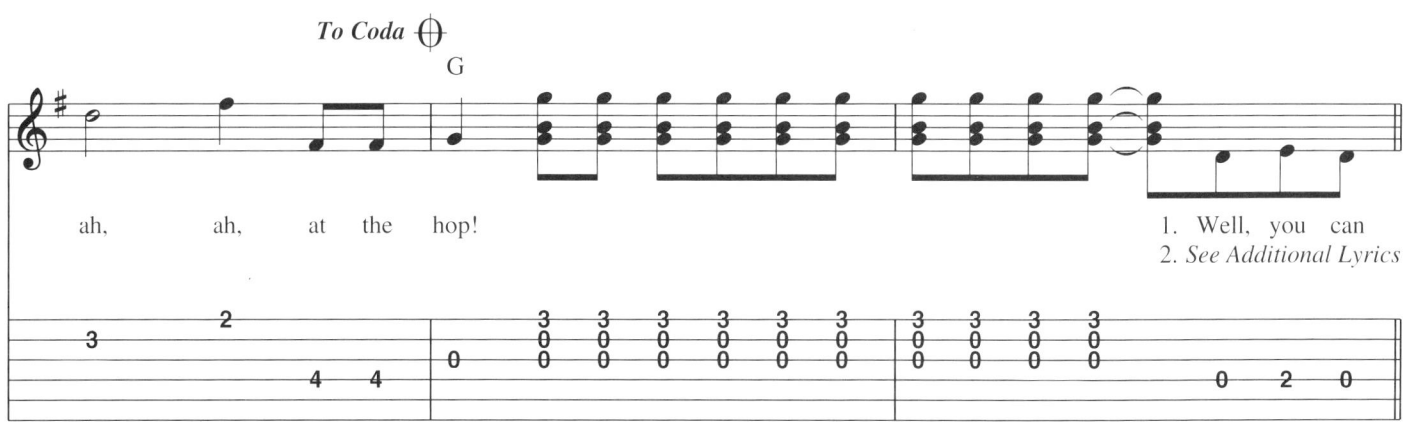

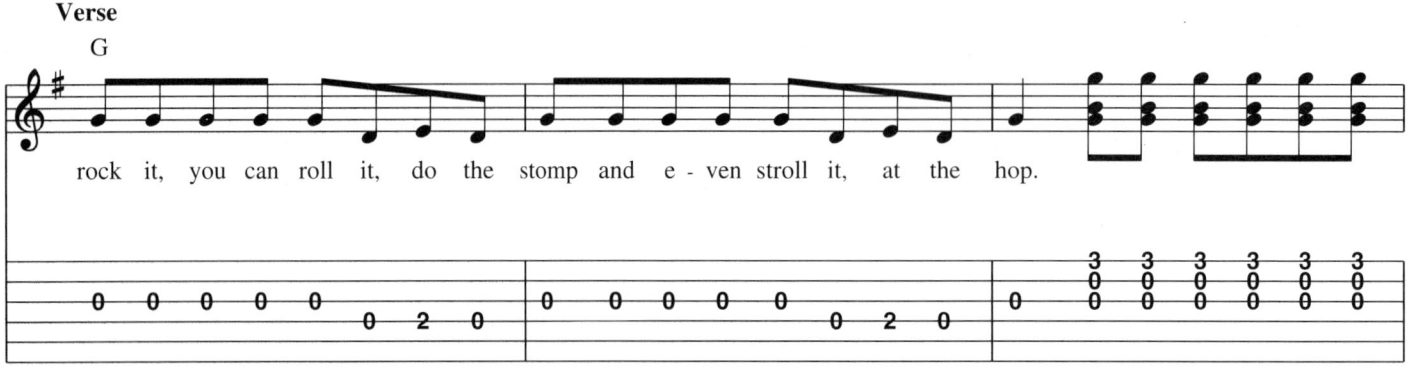
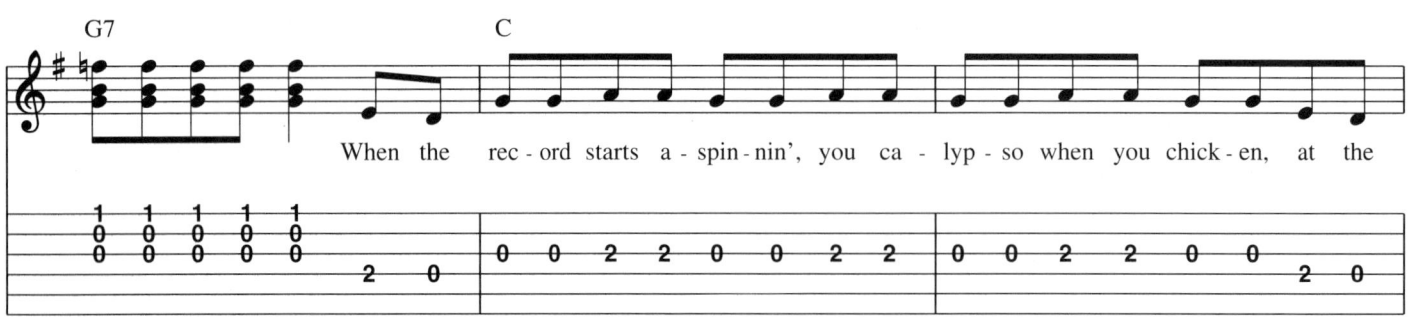
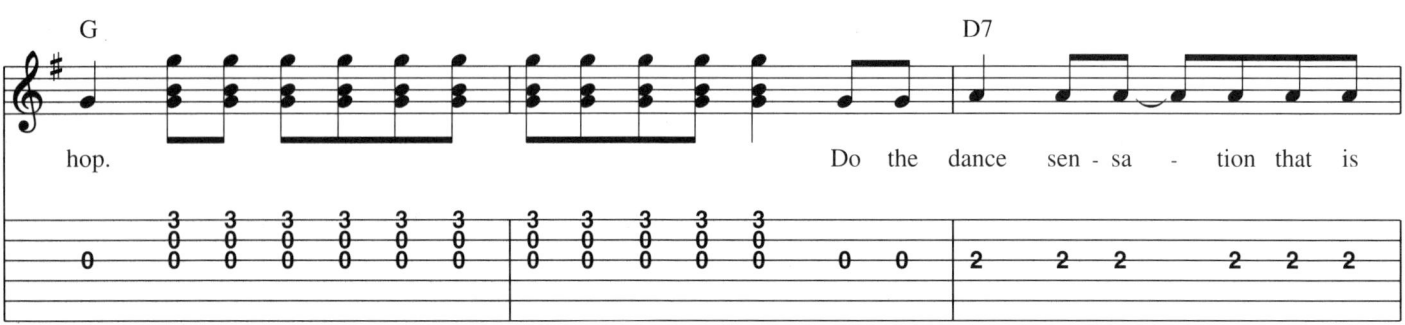
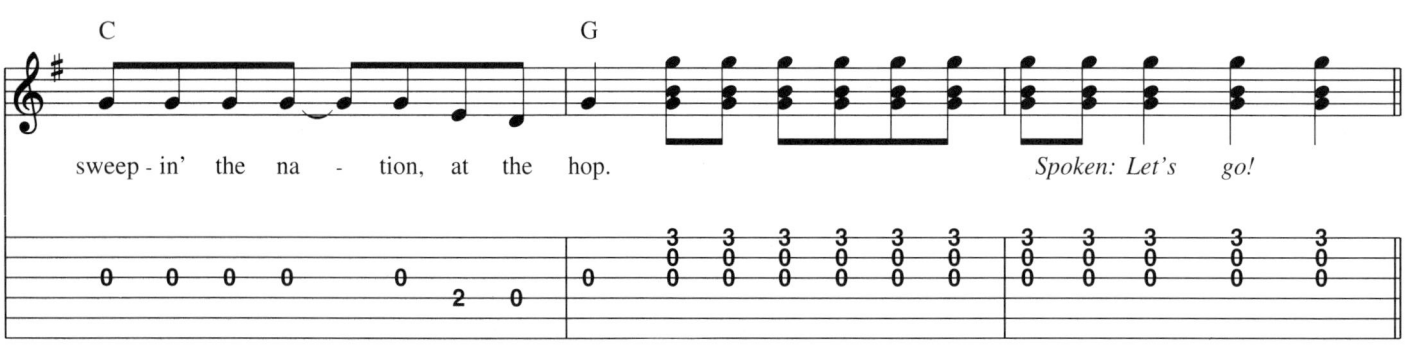

Chorus

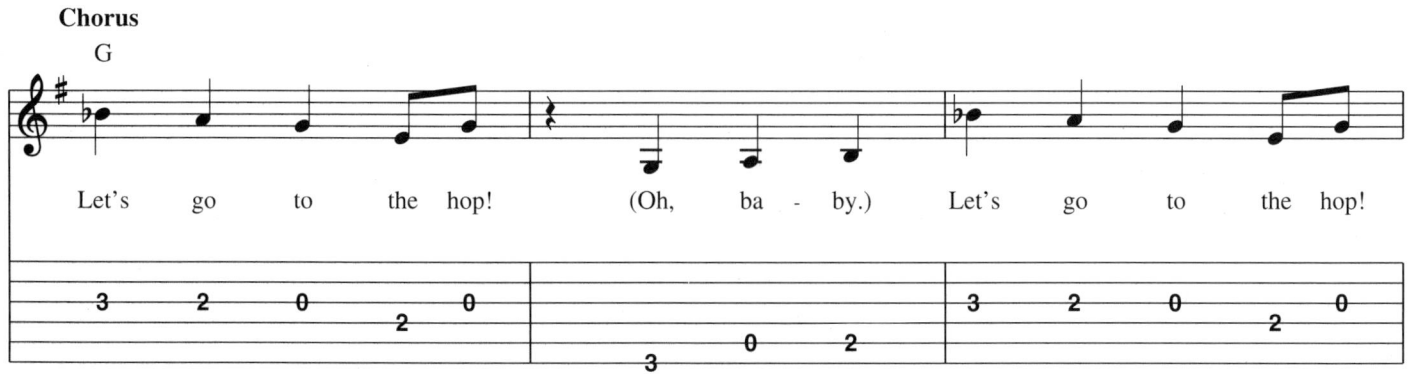

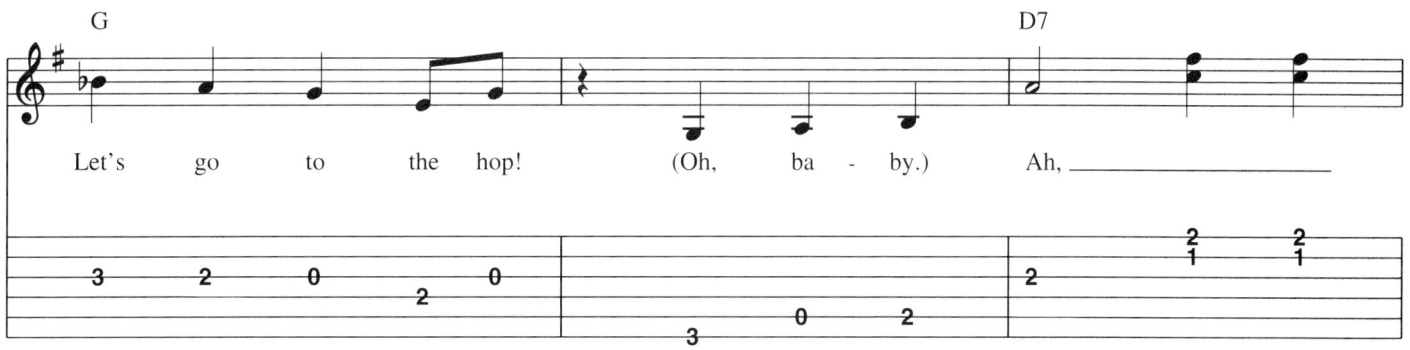

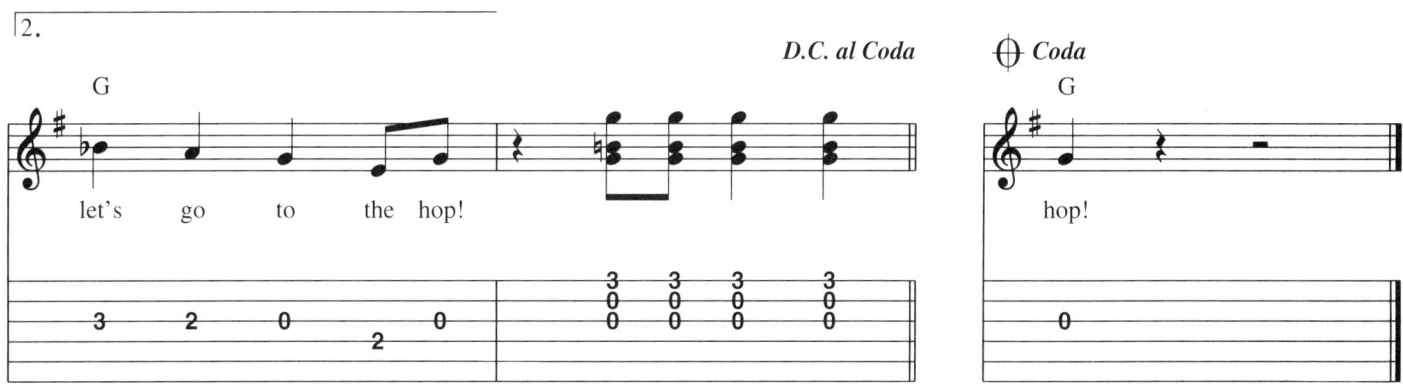

Additional Lyrics

2. Well, you can swing it, you can groove it,
   You can really start to move it, at the hop.
   Where the jumpin' is the smoothest
   And the music is the coolest, at the hop.
   All the cats and the chicks can get their kicks, at the hop.

Blue Suede Shoes

Words and Music by Carl Lee Perkins

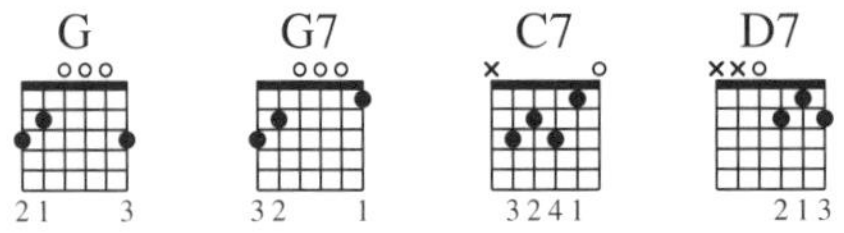

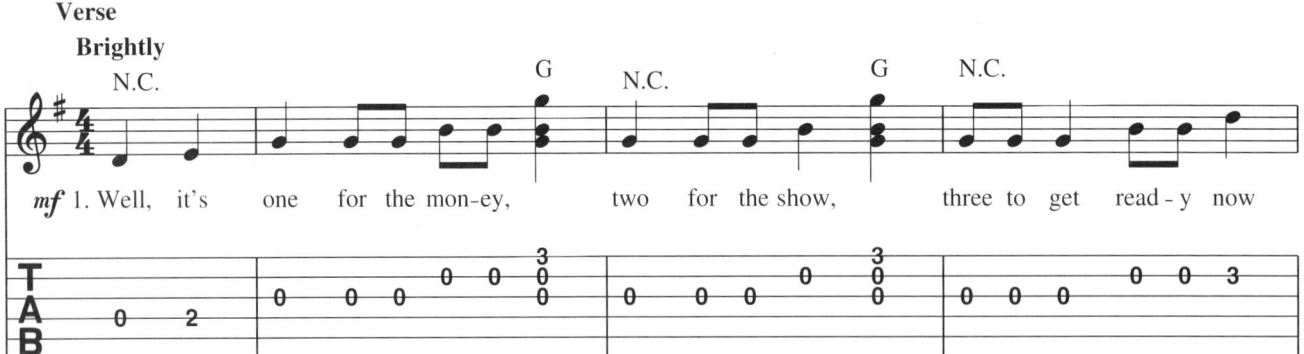

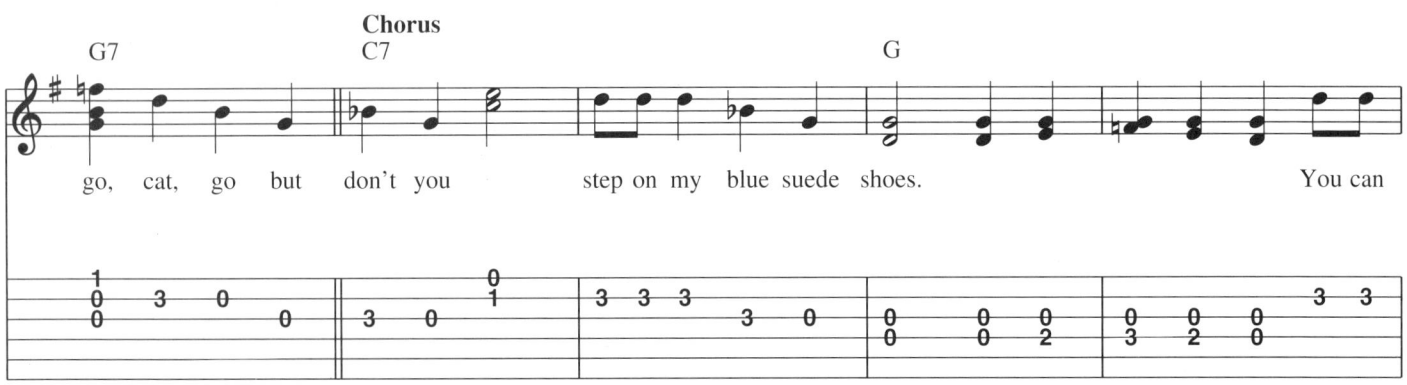

Strum Pattern: 2, 3
Pick Pattern: 3, 4

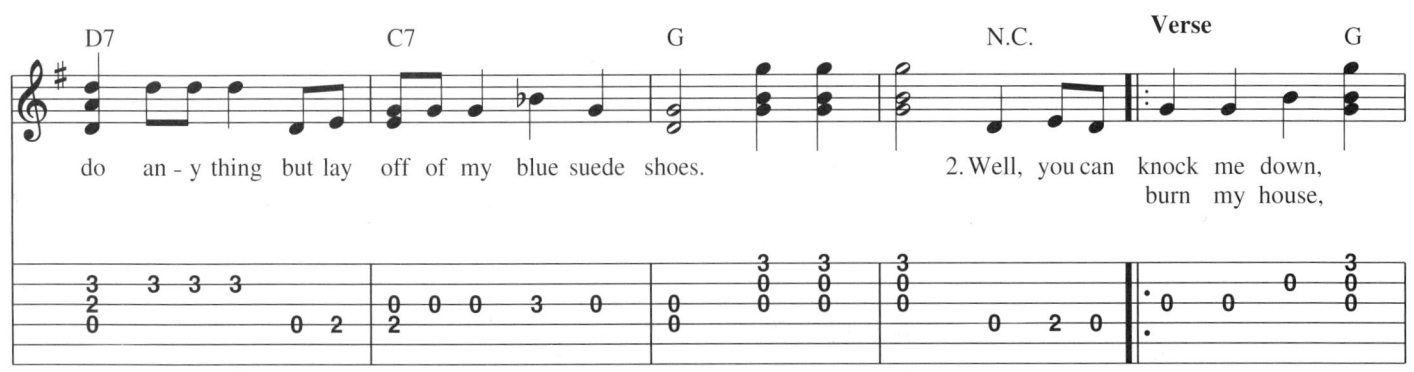

Copyright © 1955 by Carl Perkins Music, Inc.
Copyright Renewed
This arrangement Copyright © 1995 by Carl Perkins Music, Inc.
All Rights Administered by Unichappell Music Inc.
International Copyright Secured All Rights Reserved

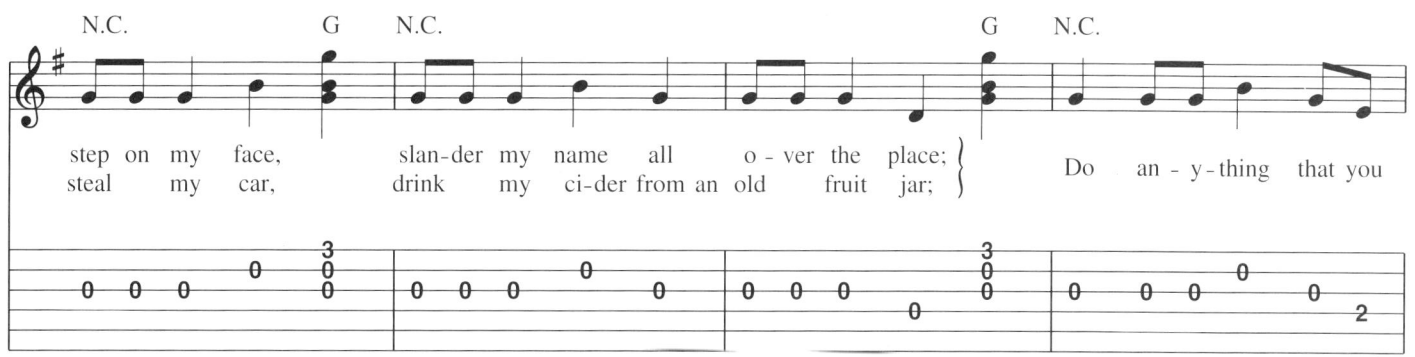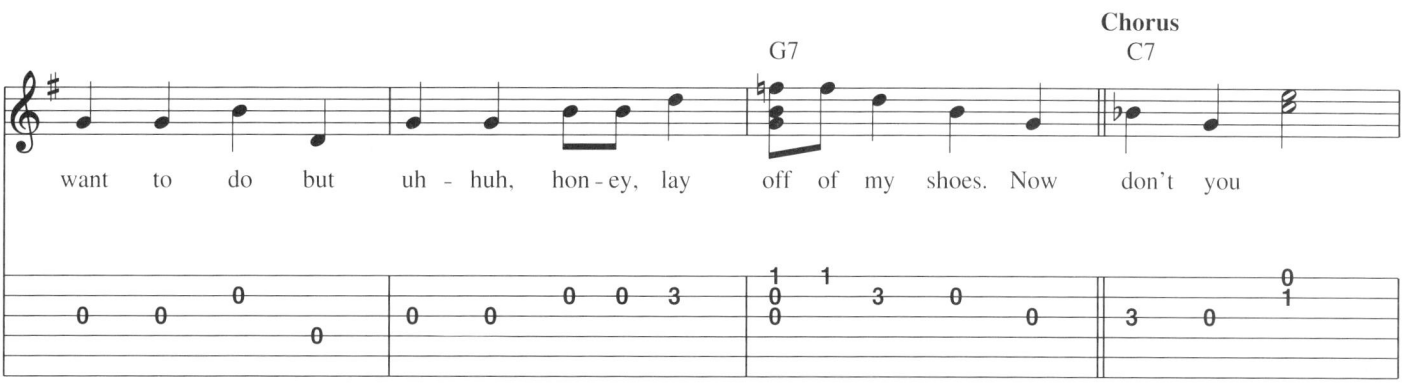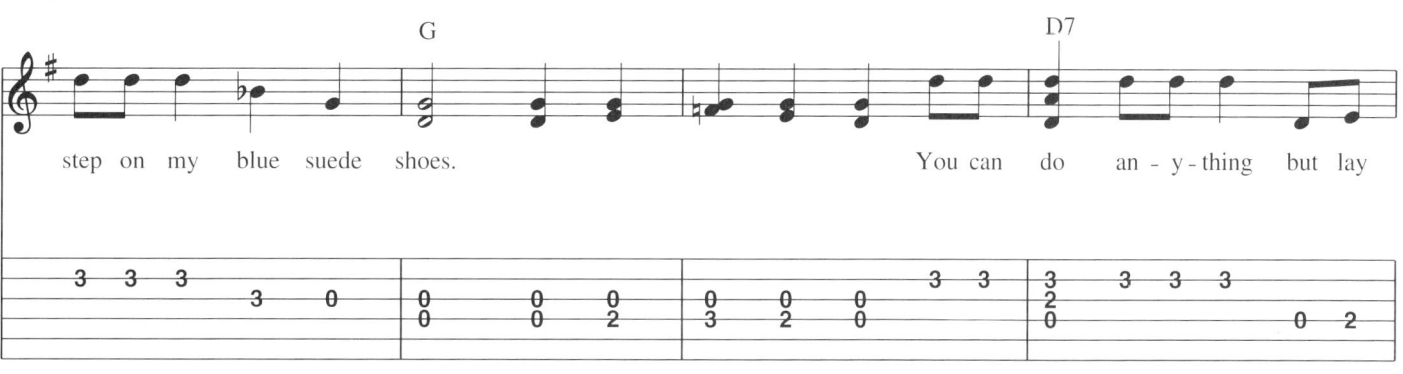

Dizzy Miss Lizzie

Words and Music by Larry Williams

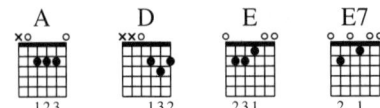

Strum Pattern: 1
Pick Pattern: 1

Intro
Moderate Rock

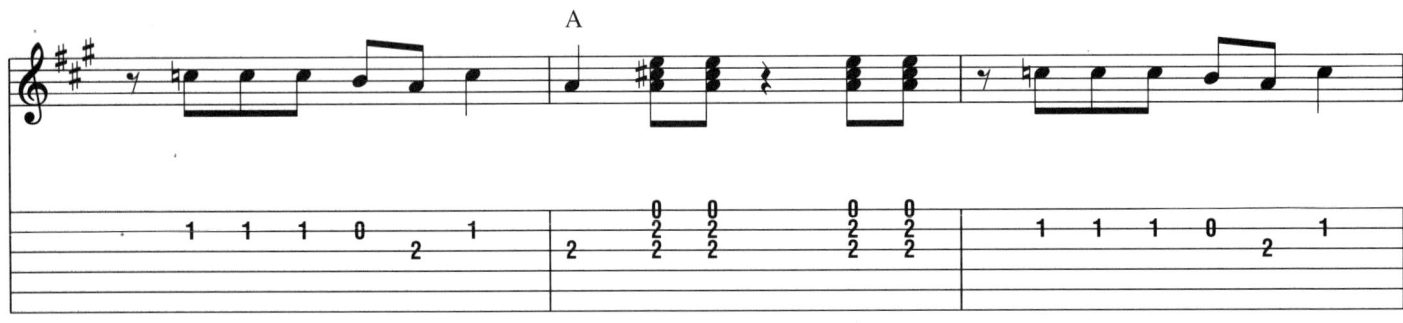

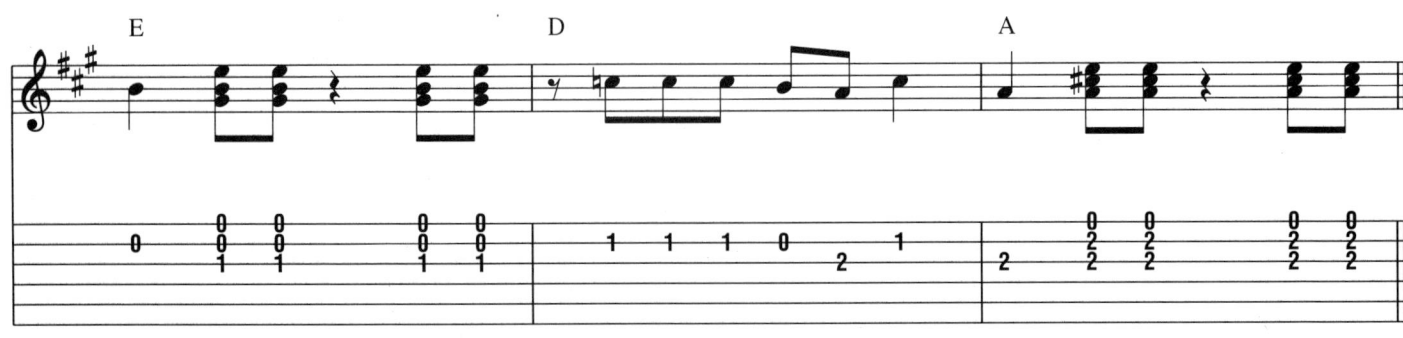

Copyright © 1958 Venice Music
Copyright Renewed by Arc Music Corp. for the United States
International Copyright Secured   All Rights Reserved

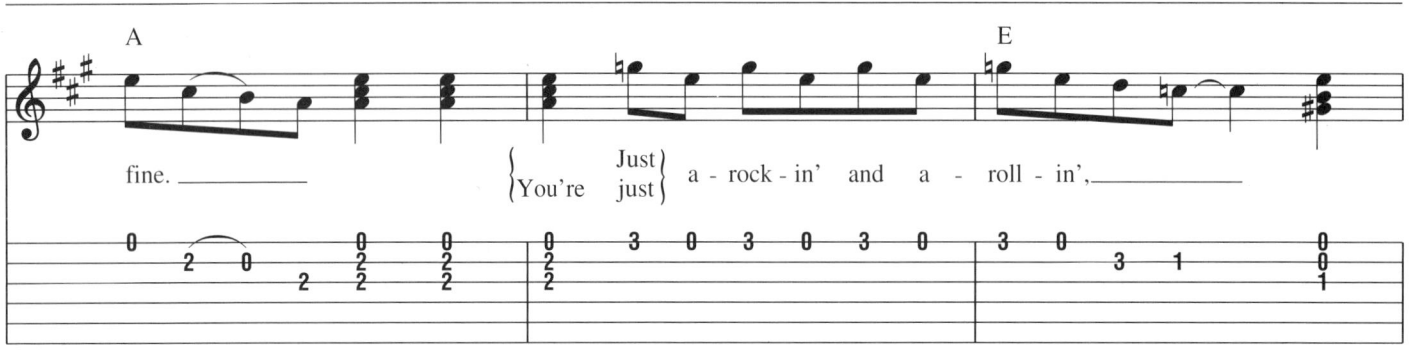

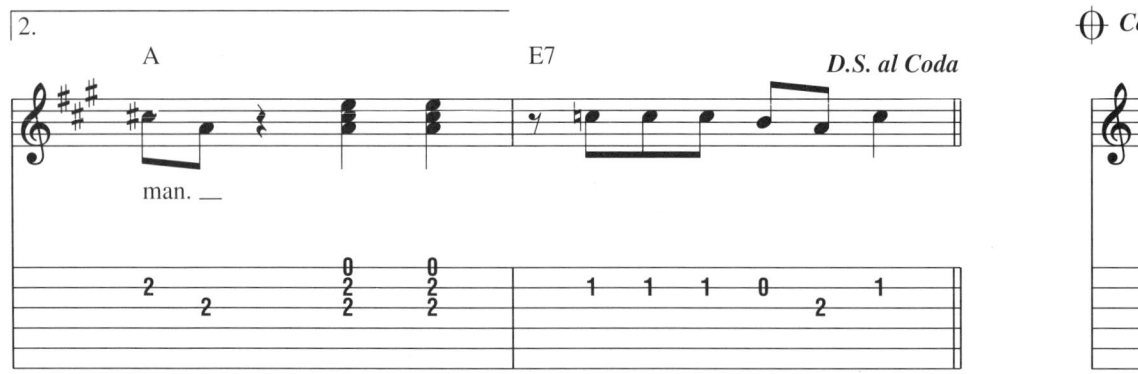

Additional Lyrics

2. You make me dizzy, Miss Lizzie,
   When you call my name.
   Woo, baby, say you're driving me insane.
   Come on, come on, come on, come on, baby,
   I wanna be your lovin' man.

3. Run and tell your mama
   I want you to be my bride.
   Run and tell your brother.
   Baby, don't run and hide.
   You make me dizzy, Miss Lizzie,
   Girl, I wanna marry you.

Don't Be Cruel
(To A Heart That's True)

Words and Music by Otis Blackwell and Elvis Presley

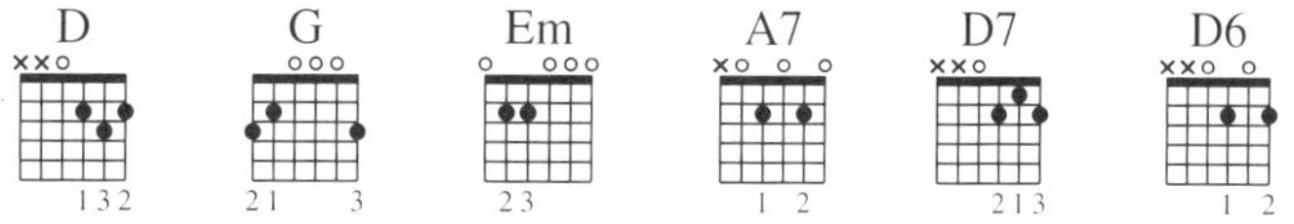

Strum Pattern: 3, 4
Pick Pattern: 3, 5

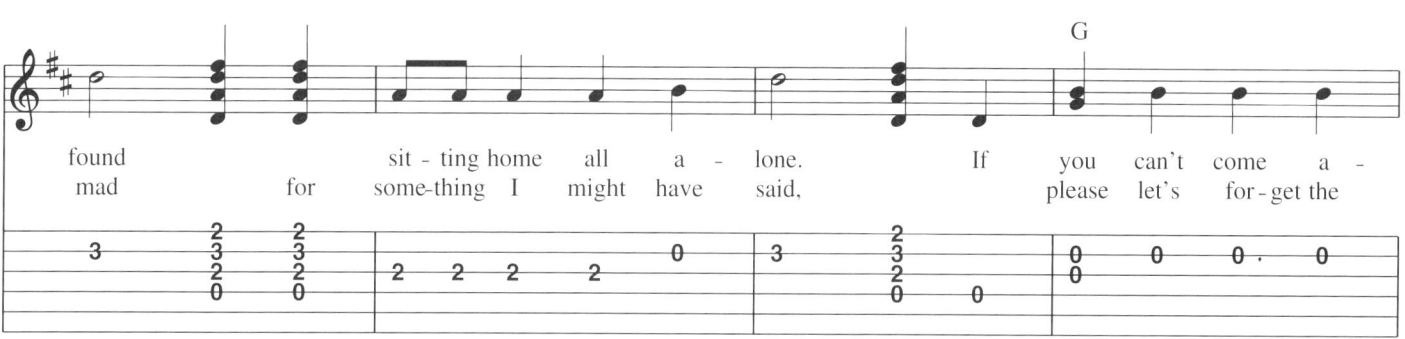

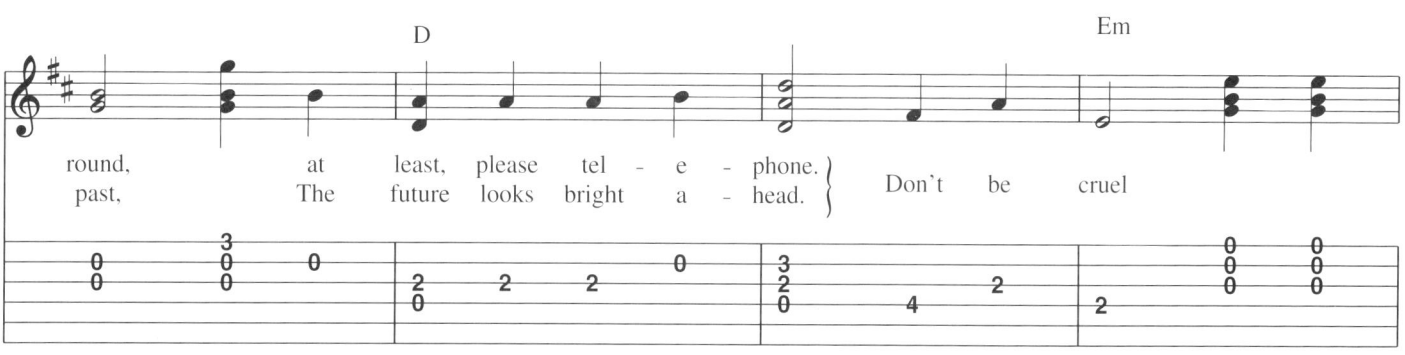

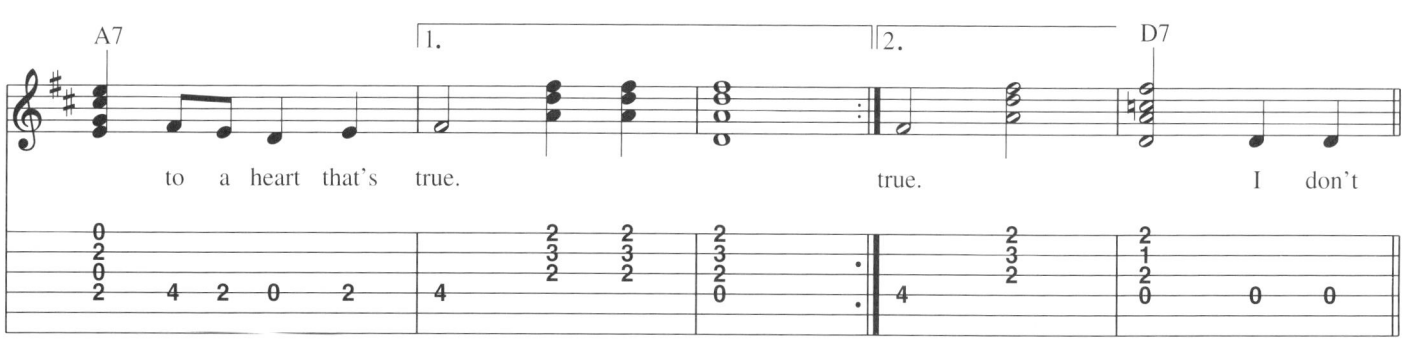

Copyright © 1956 by Unart Music Corporation and Elvis Presley Music, Inc.
Copyright Renewed and Assigned to Elvis Presley Music (Administered by R&H Music)
International Copyright Secured   All Rights Reserved

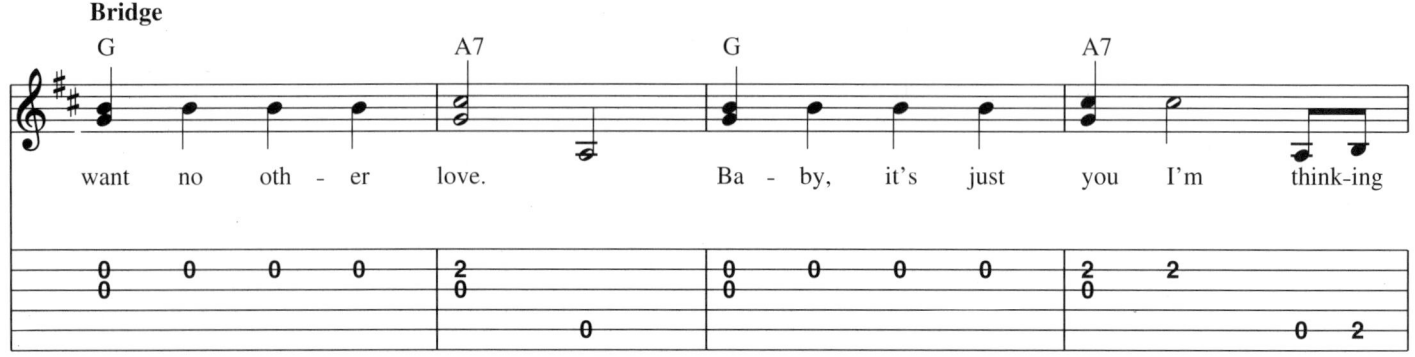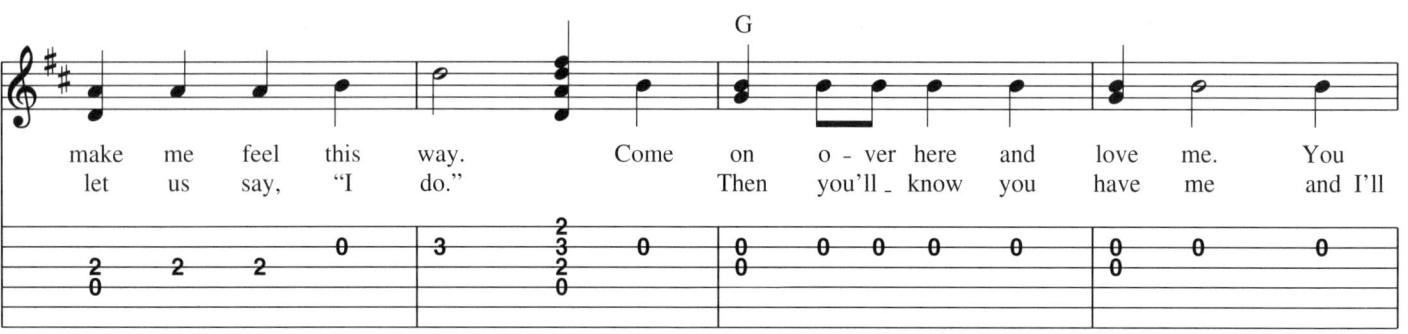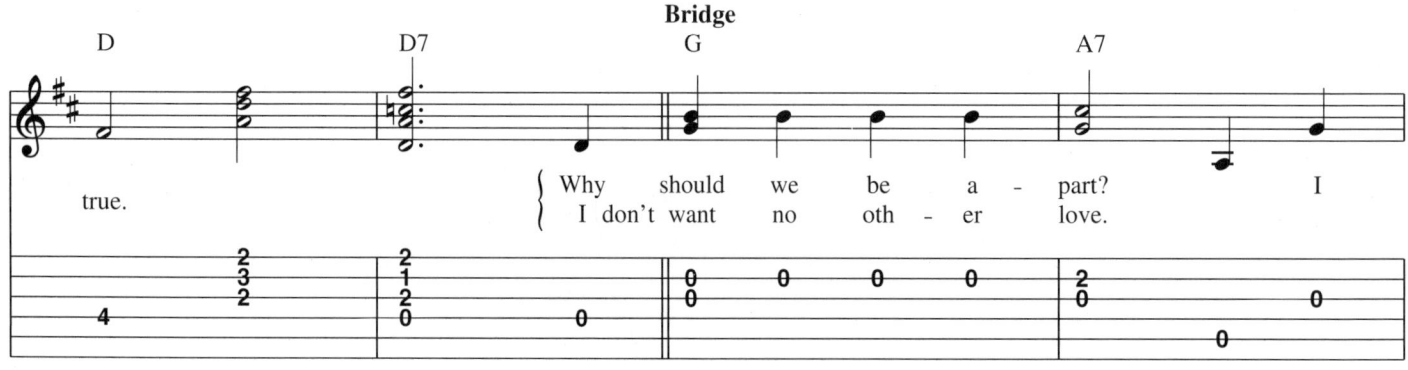

1.
G A7 D
real - ly love you ba - by, cross my heart. 4. Let's
Ba - by, it's just you I'm think - ing
2.
Em A7
of. Don't be cruel to a heart that's
D Em A7
true. Don't be cruel to a heart that's
Bridge
D7 G A7
true. I don't want no oth - er love.
G A7 D D6
Ba - by, it's just you I'm think-ing of.

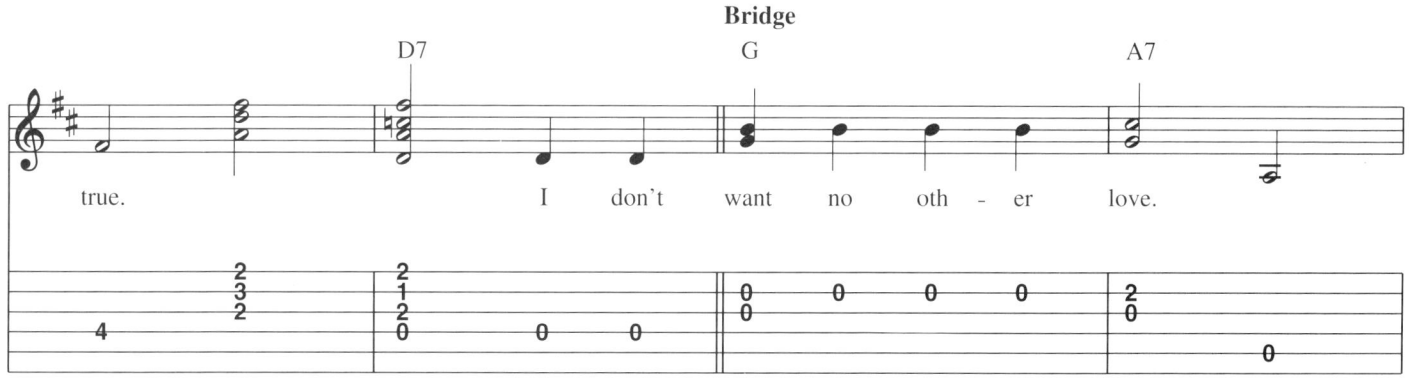

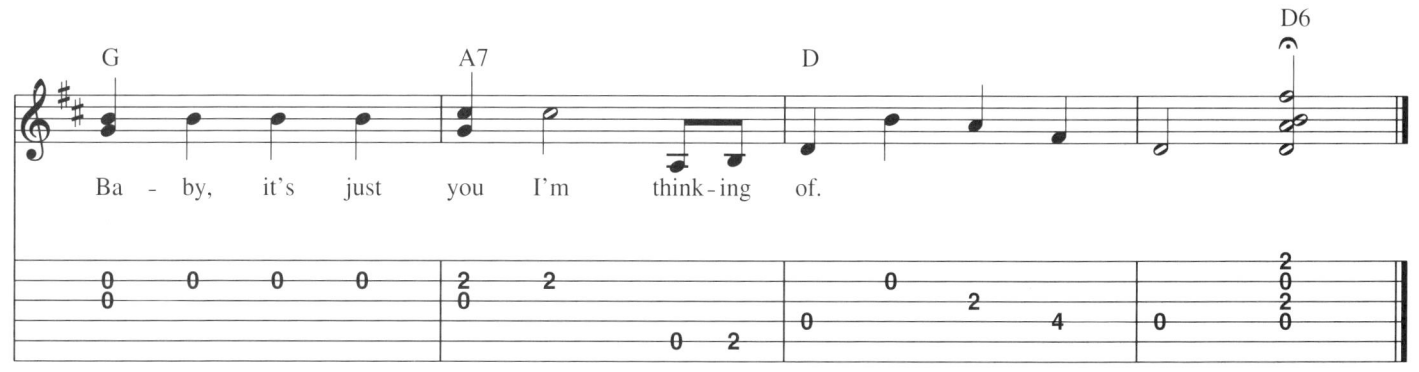

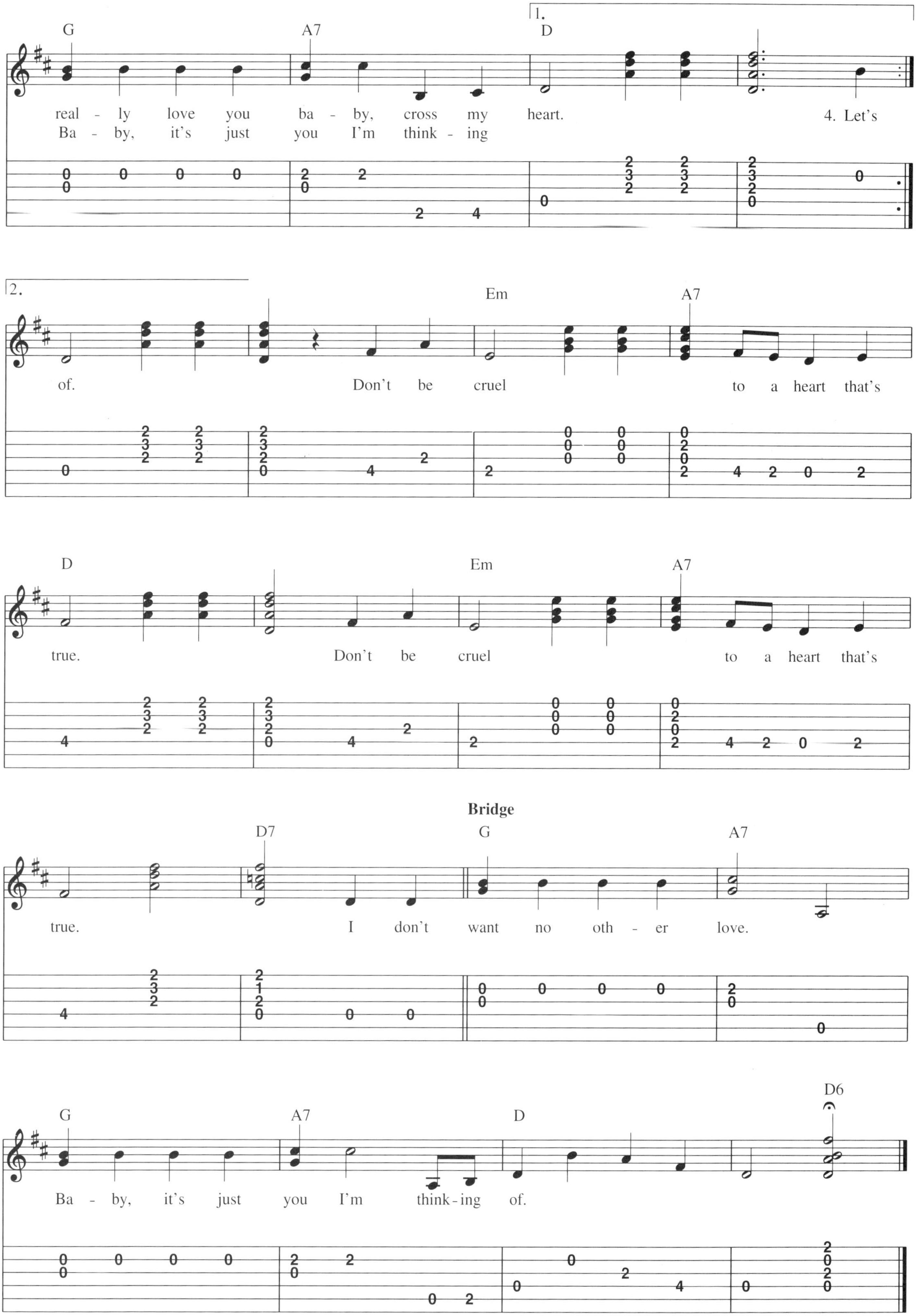

Great Balls of Fire

Words and Music by Otis Blackwell and Jack Hammer

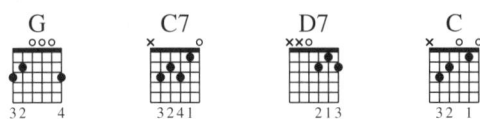

Strum Pattern: 1, 2
Pick Pattern: 2, 4

Intro
Bright Rock

You shake my nerves and you rattle my brain.
Instrumental

Too much love drives a man insane. You broke my will,

but what a thrill. Goodness gracious, great balls of fire!

Verse

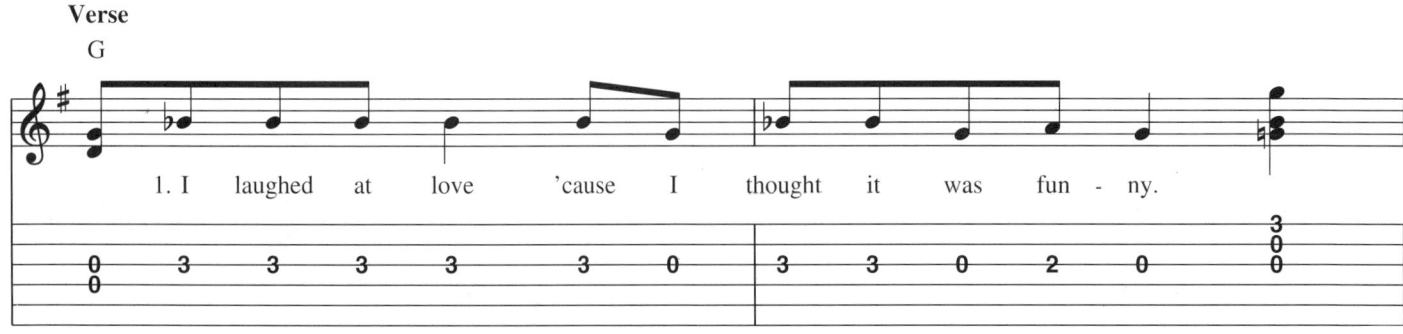

1. I laughed at love 'cause I thought it was funny.

Copyright © 1957 by Chappell & Co. and Unichappell Music Inc.
Copyright Renewed
International Copyright Secured   All Rights Reserved

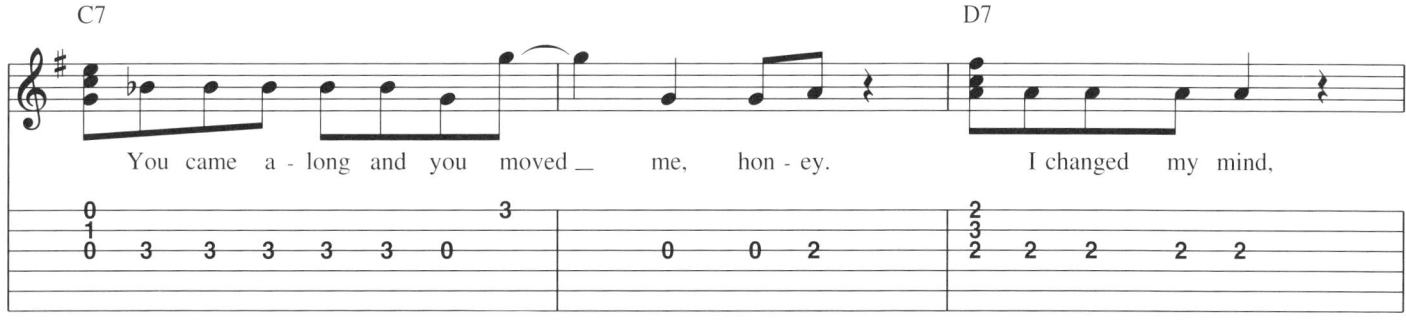

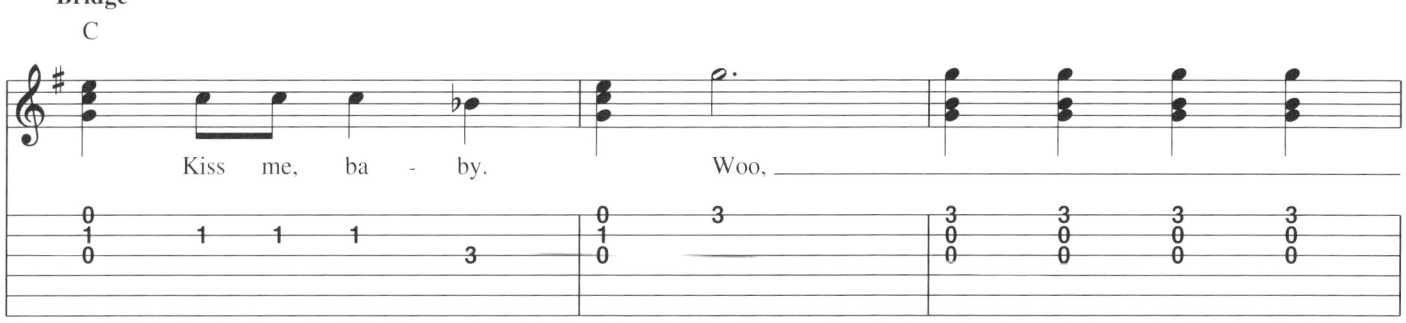

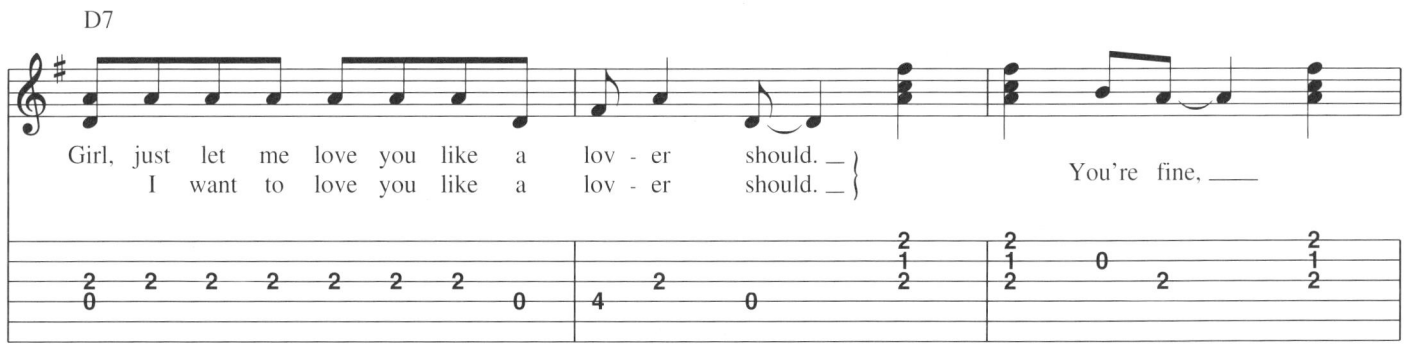

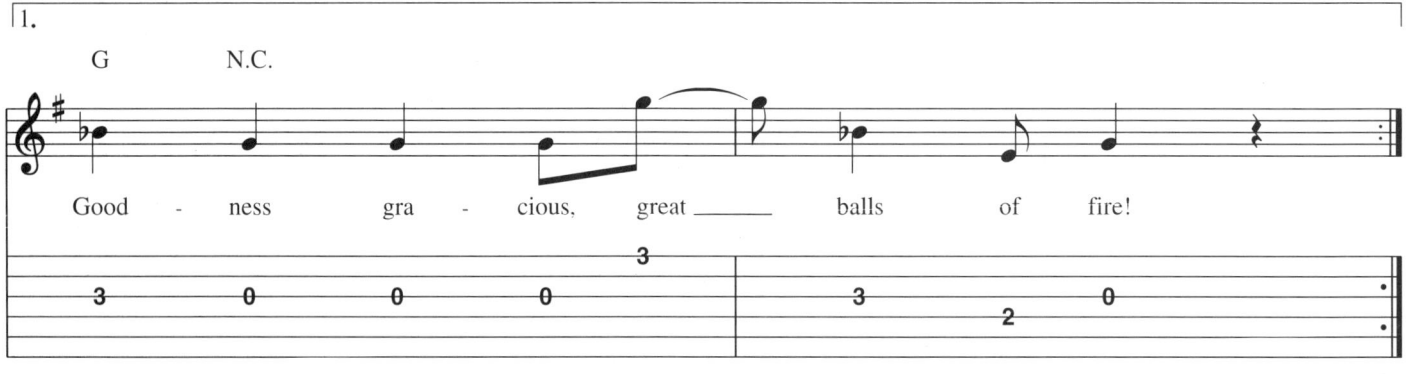
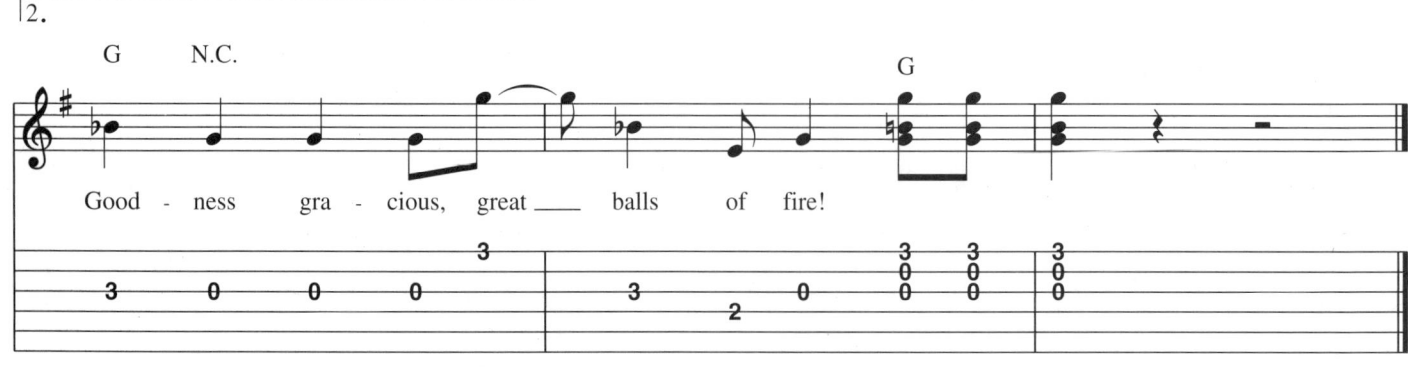

Hound Dog

Words and Music by Jerry Leiber and Mike Stoller

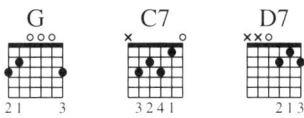

Strum Pattern: 2, 5
Pick Pattern: 4

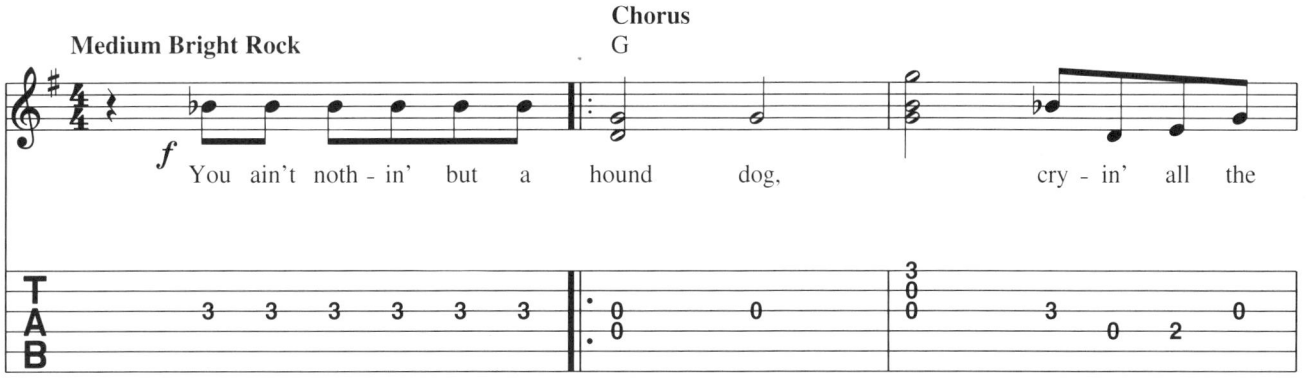

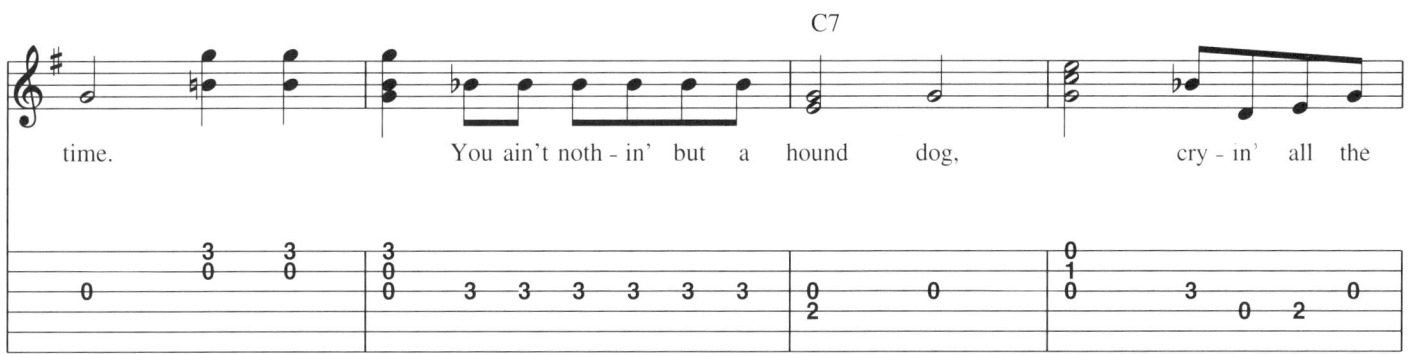

Copyright © 1956 by Elvis Presley Music, Inc. and Lion Publishing Co., Inc.
Copyright Renewed, Assigned to Gladys Music (Administered by Williamson Music)
and MCA Music Publishing, A Division of UNIVERSAL STUDIOS, INC.
This arrangement Copyright © 1996 Gladys Music and MCA Music Publishing, A Division of UNIVERSAL STUDIOS, INC.
International Copyright Secured   All Rights Reserved

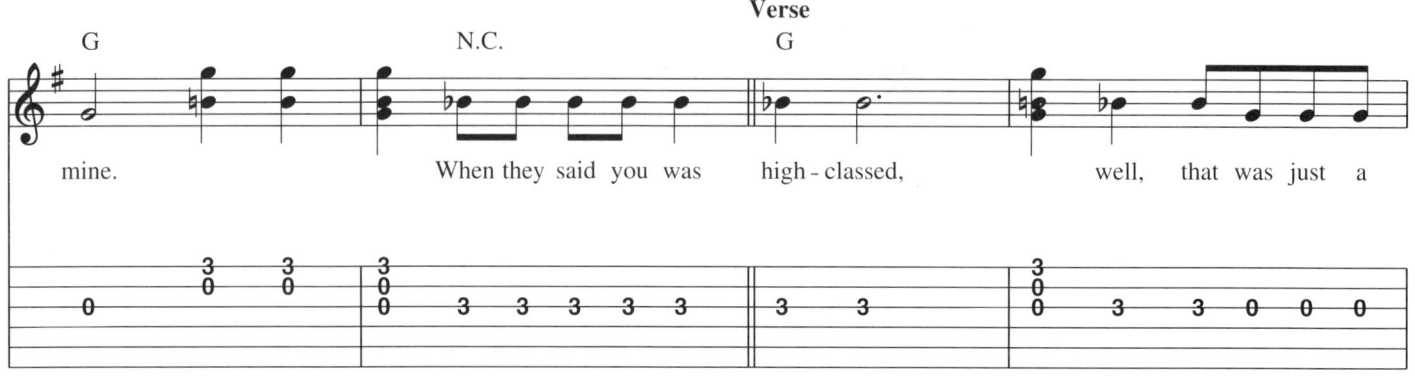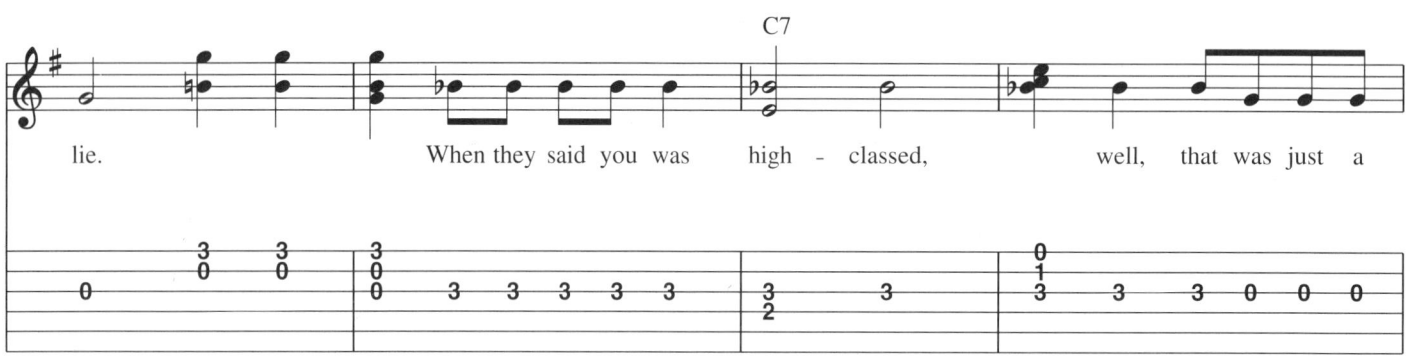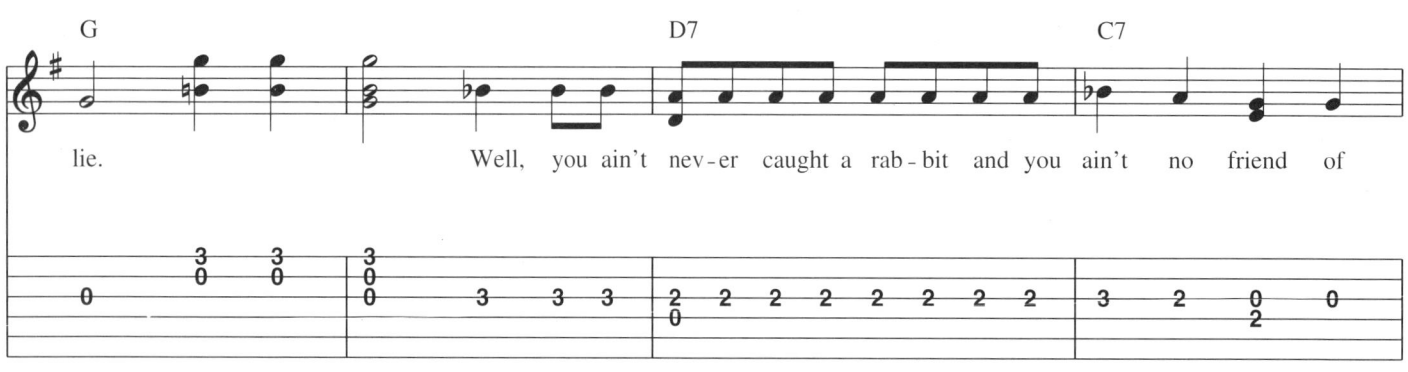

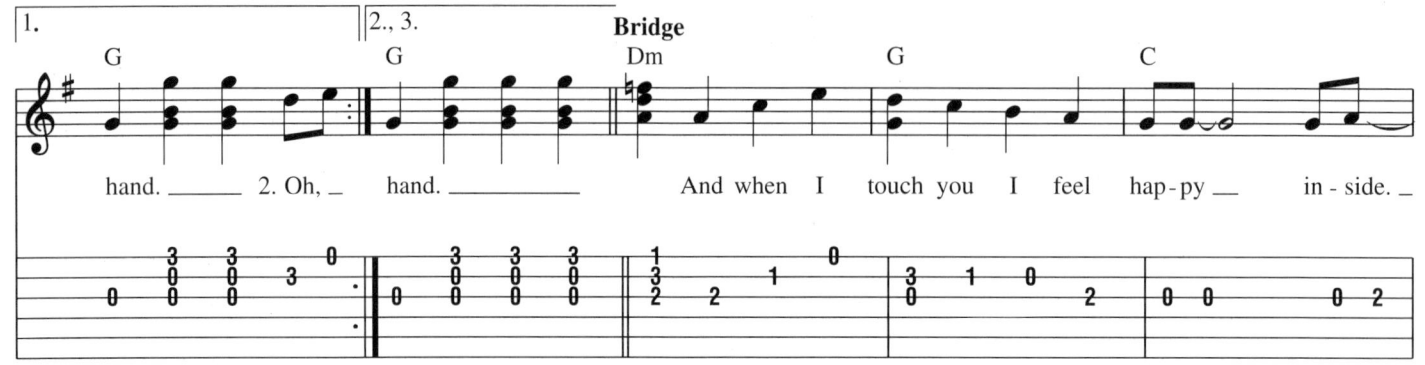
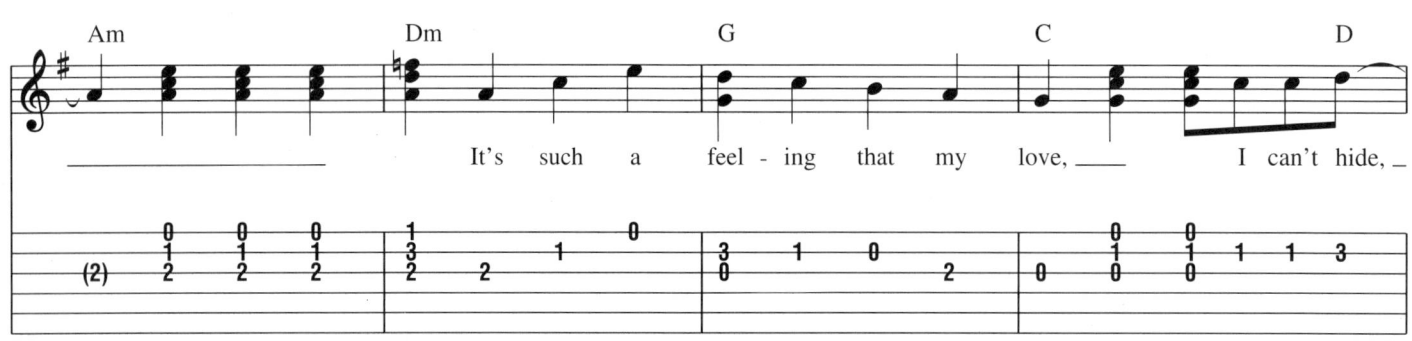

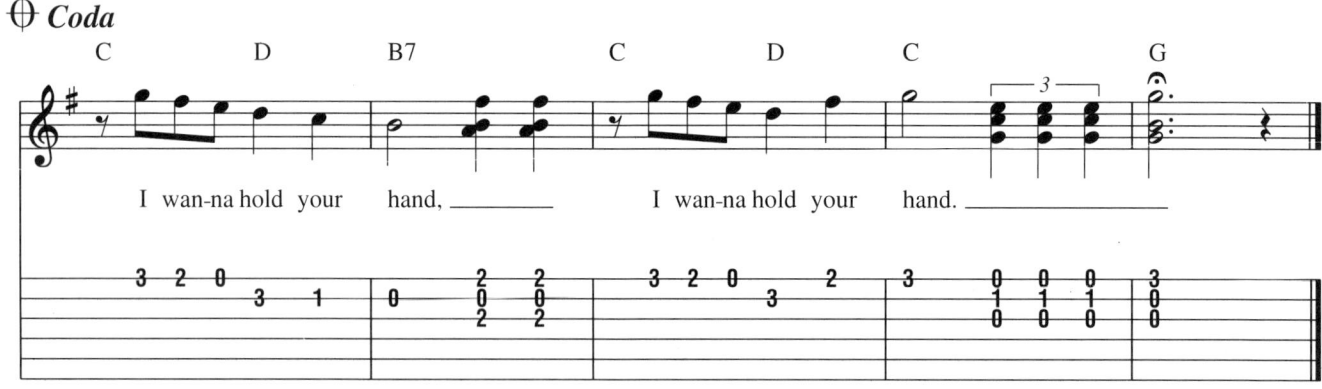

Additional Lyrics

2. Oh, please say to me
   You'll let me be your man.
   And please say to me
   You'll let me hold your hand.

3. Yeah, you got that somethin',
   I think you'll understand.
   When I {say/feel} that something,
   I wanna hold your hand.

Strum Pattern: 3
Pick Pattern: 3

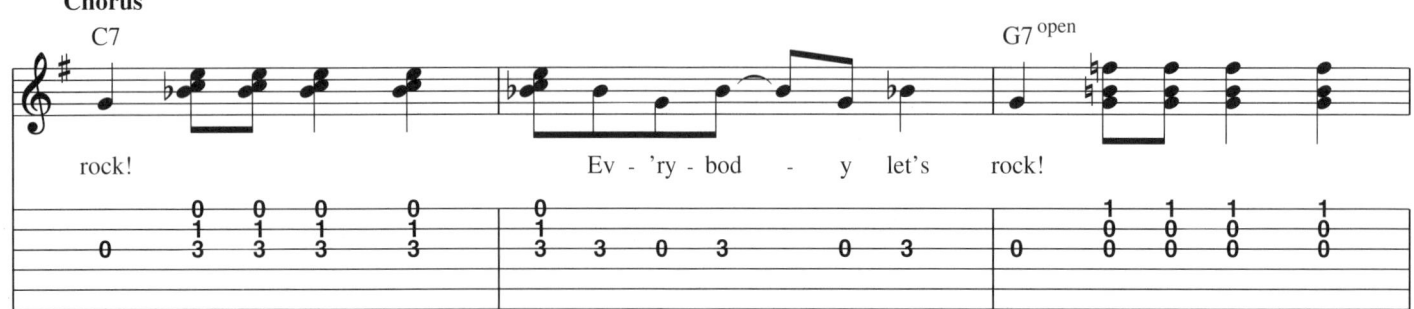

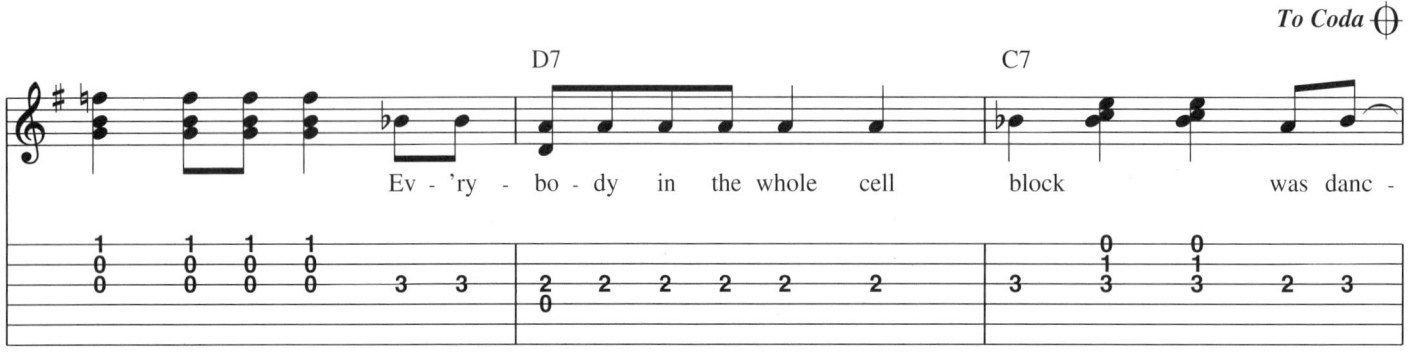

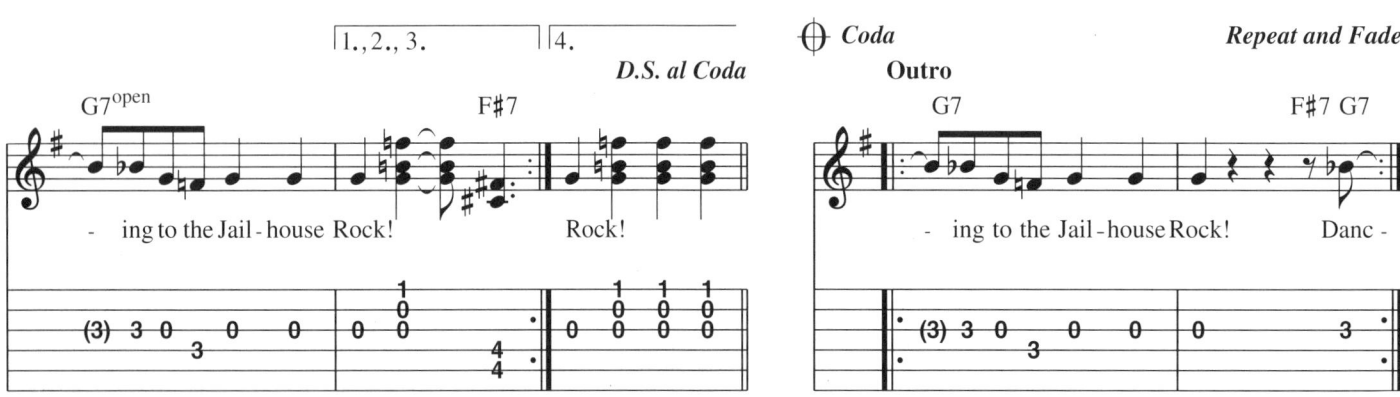

Additional Lyrics

2. Spider Murphy played the tenor saxophone,
   Little Joe was blowin' on the slide trombone.
   The drummer boy from Illinois went crash, boom, bang;
   The whole rhythm section was the Purple Gang.

3. Number Forty-seven said to number Three:
   "You're the cutest jailbird I ever did see.
   I sure would be delighted with your company,
   Come on and do the Jailhouse Rock with me."

4. The sad sack was a-sittin' on a block of stone,
   Way over in the corner weeping all alone.
   The warden said: "Hey, Buddy, don't you be no square,
   If you can't find a partner, use a wooden chair!"

5. Shifty Henry said to Bugs: "For heaven's sake,
   No one's lookin', now's our chance to make a break."
   Bugsy turned to Shifty and he said: "Nix, nix;
   I wanna stick around a while and get my kicks."

Johnny B. Goode

Words and Music by Chuck Berry

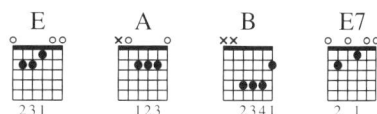

Strum Pattern: 1, 6
Pick Pattern: 4, 5

Intro
Bright Rock Beat

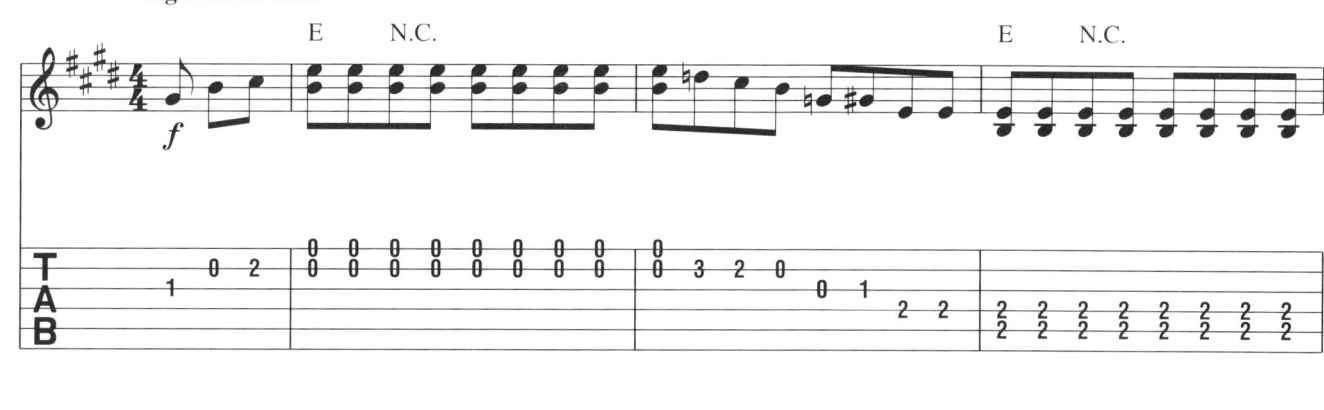

1. Deep

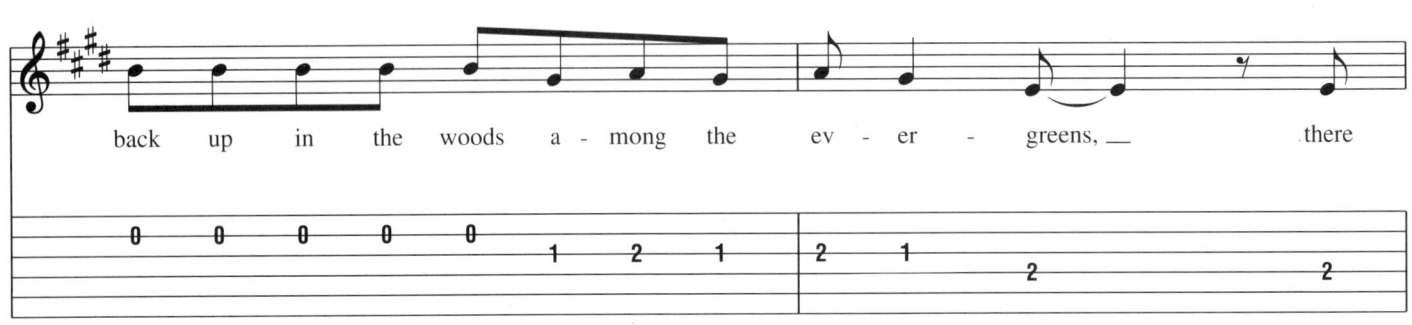

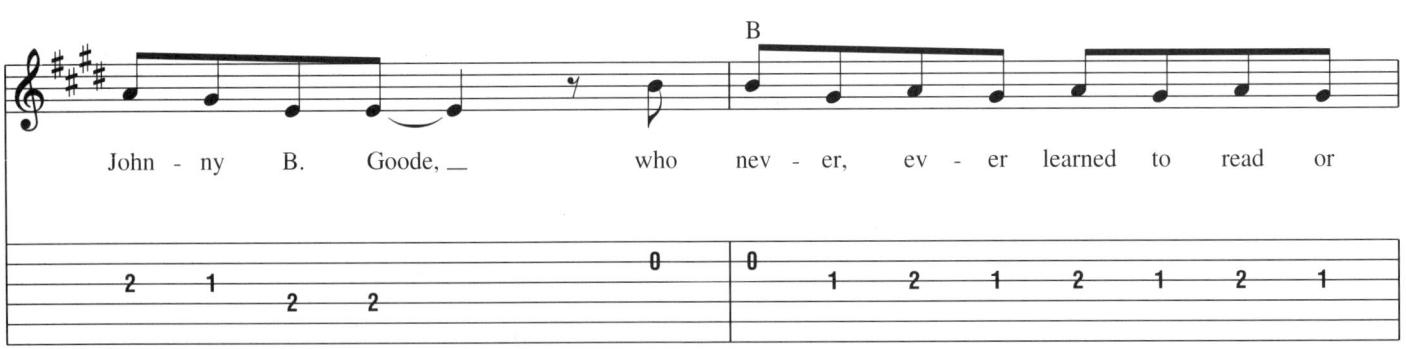
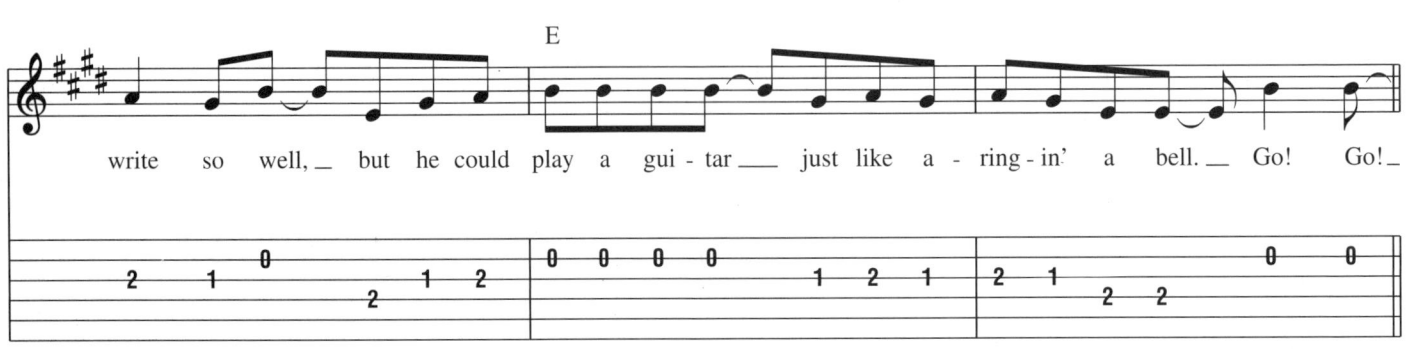

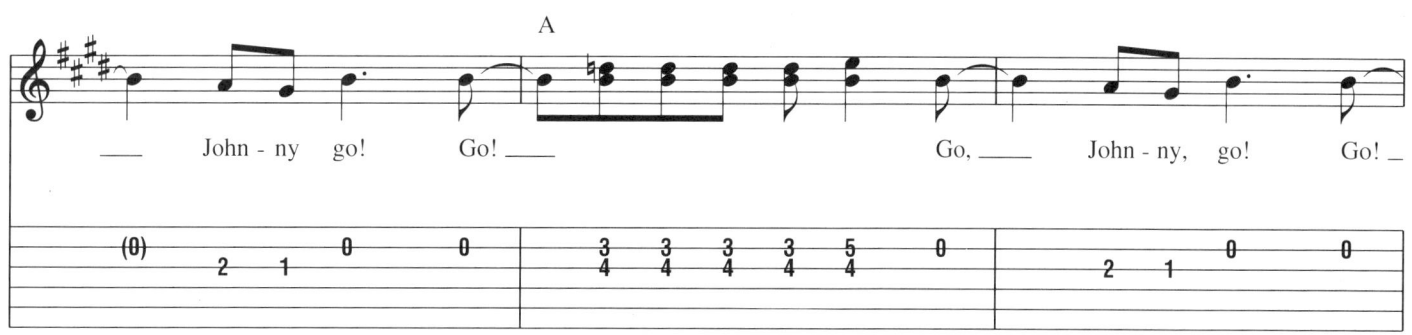
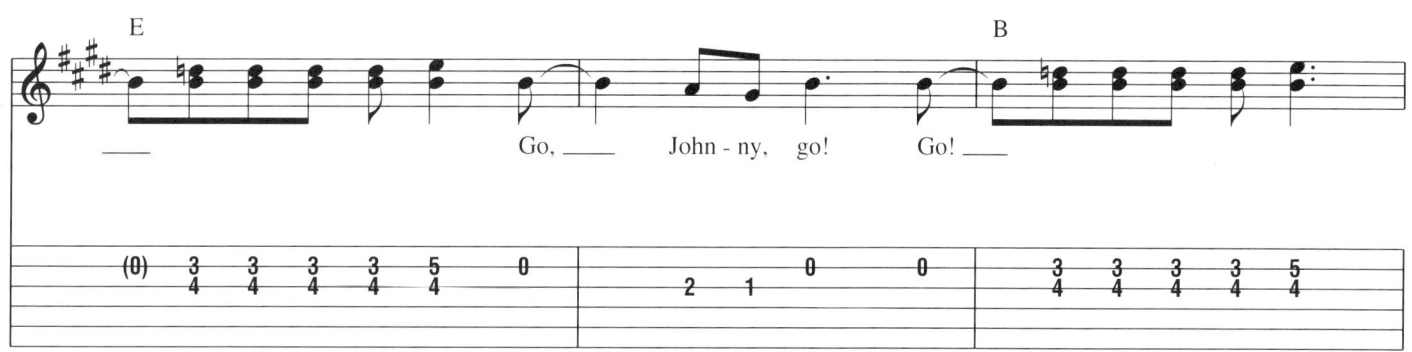

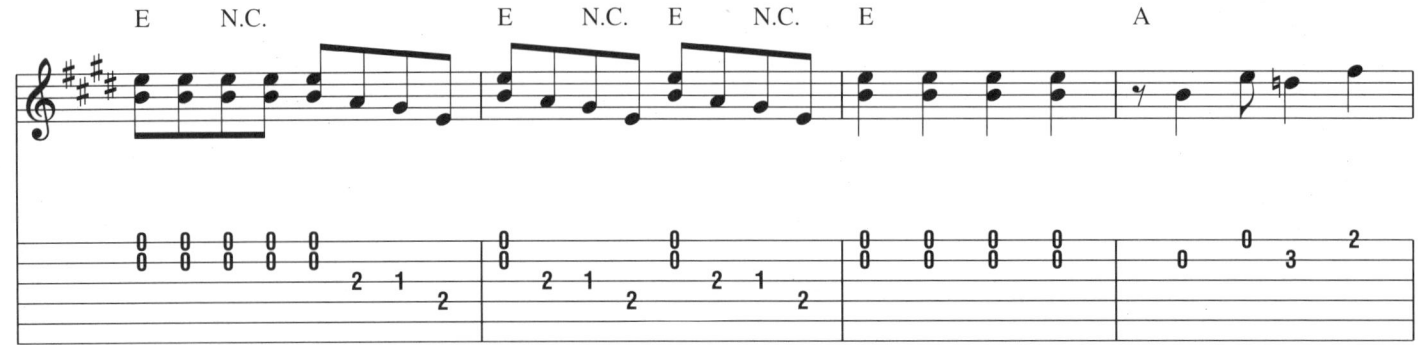

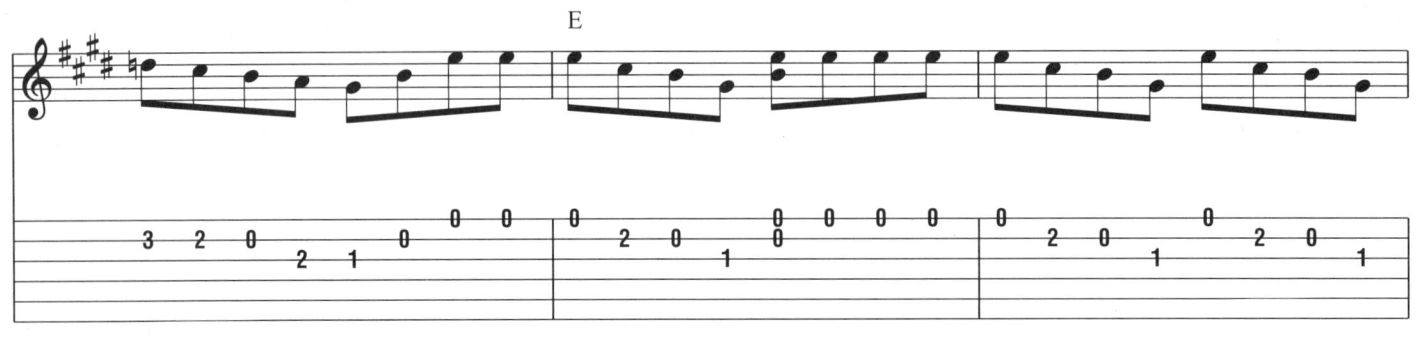

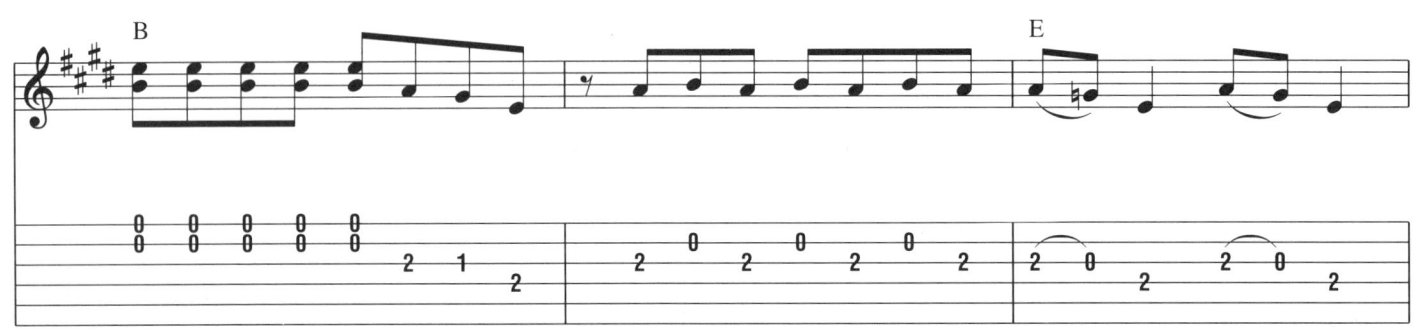

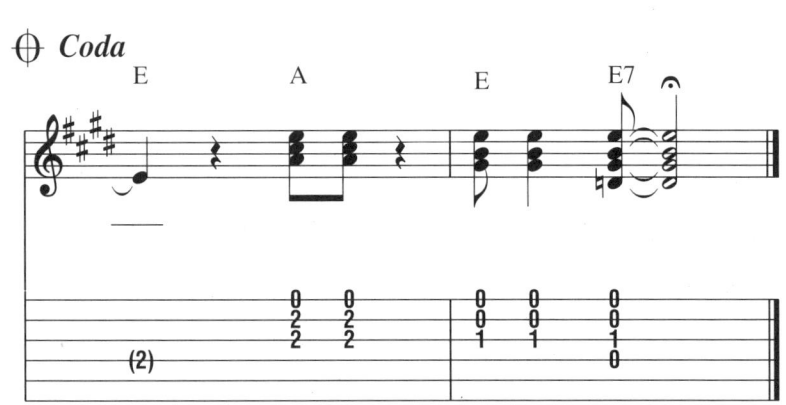

Additional Lyrics

2. He used to carry his guitar in a gunny sack,
   Go sit beneath the tree by the railroad track.
   Old engineers would see him sittin' in the shade,
   Strummin' with the rhythm that the drivers made.
   When people passed by him they would stop and say,
   "Oh my, but that little country boy could play."

3. His mother told him, "Someday you will be a man,
   And you will be the leader of a big ol' band.
   Many people comin' from miles around
   Will hear you play your music when the sun go down.
   Maybe some day your name will be in lights,
   Sayin', "Johnny B. Goode tonight."

Long Tall Sally

Words and Music by Enotris Johnson, Richard Penniman and Robert Blackwell

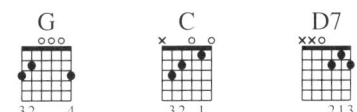

Strum Pattern: 1
Pick Pattern: 2

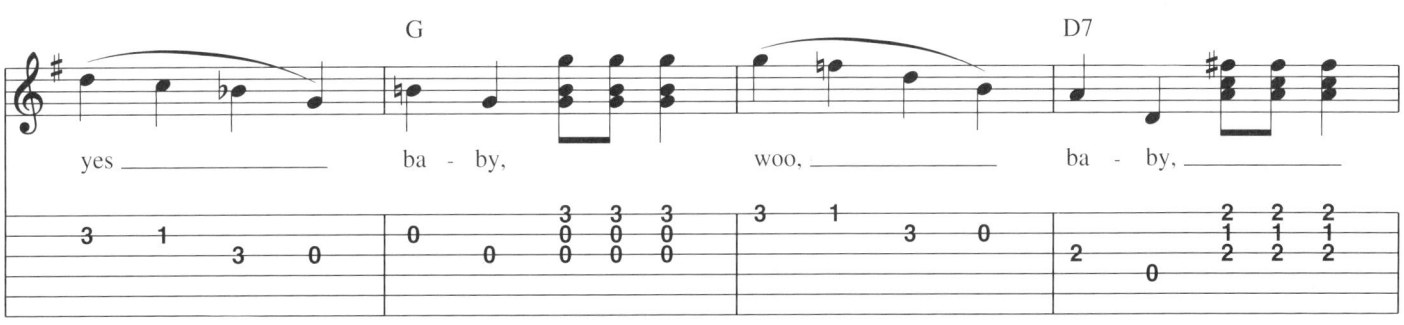

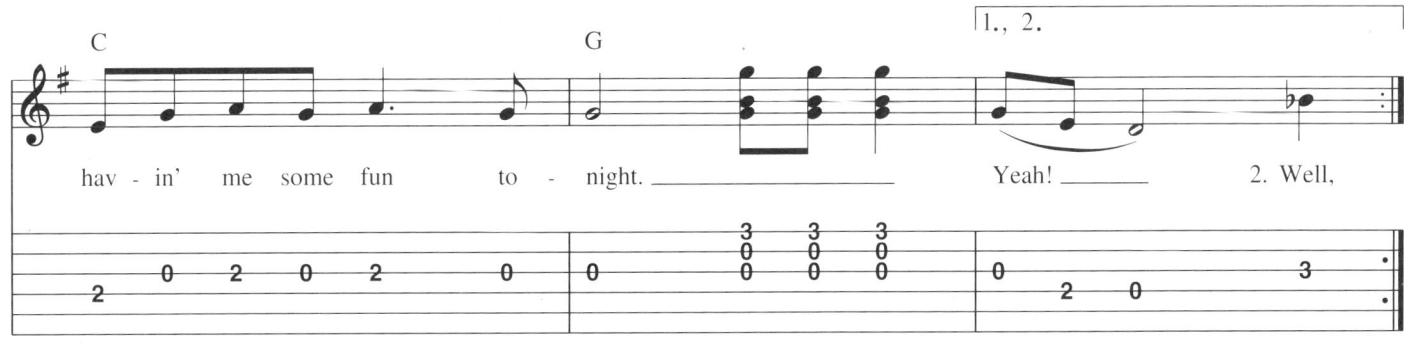

© 1956 VENICE MUSIC CORP.
Copyright Renewed
All Rights Controlled and Administered by EMI BLACKWOOD MUSIC INC. under license from SONY/ATV SONGS LLC
All Rights Reserved   International Copyright Secured   Used by Permission

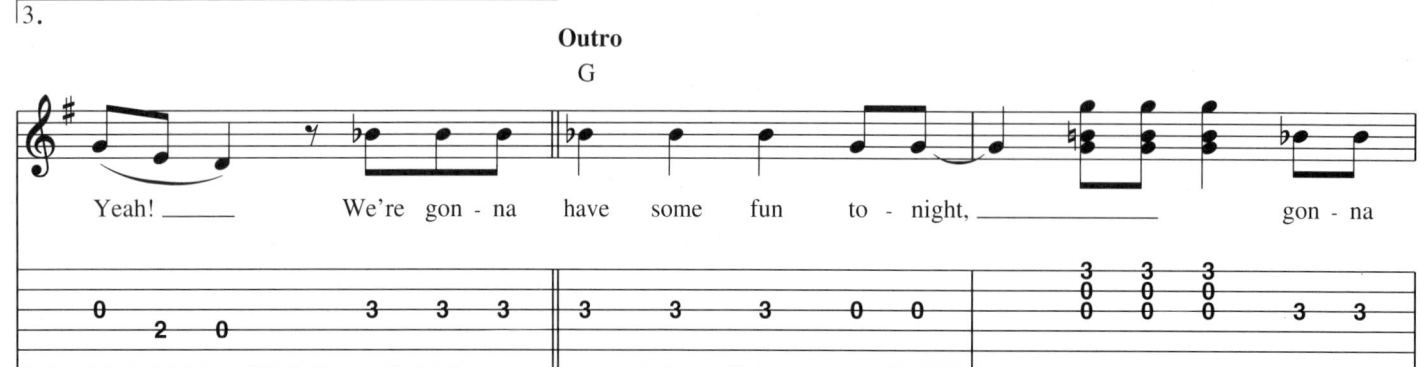

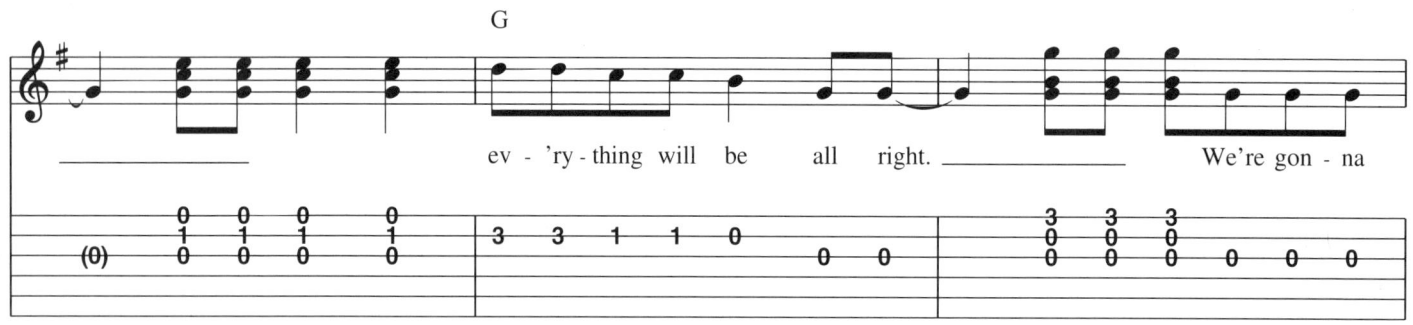
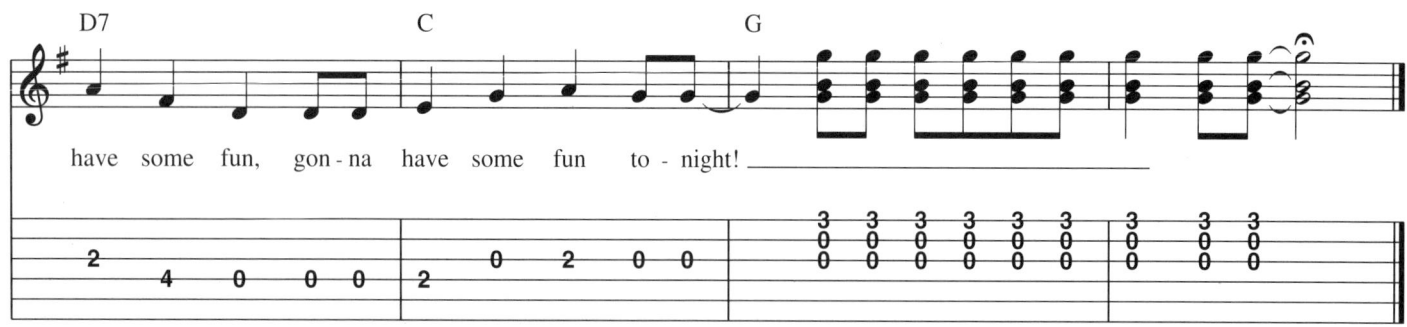

Additional Lyrics

2. Well, Long Tall Sally has a lot on the ball,
   And nobody cares if she's long and tall.

3. Well, I saw Uncle John with Long Tall Sally,
   He saw Aunt Mary comin' and he ducked back in the alley.

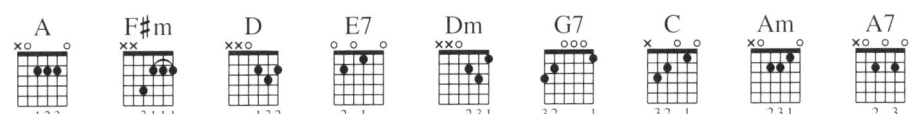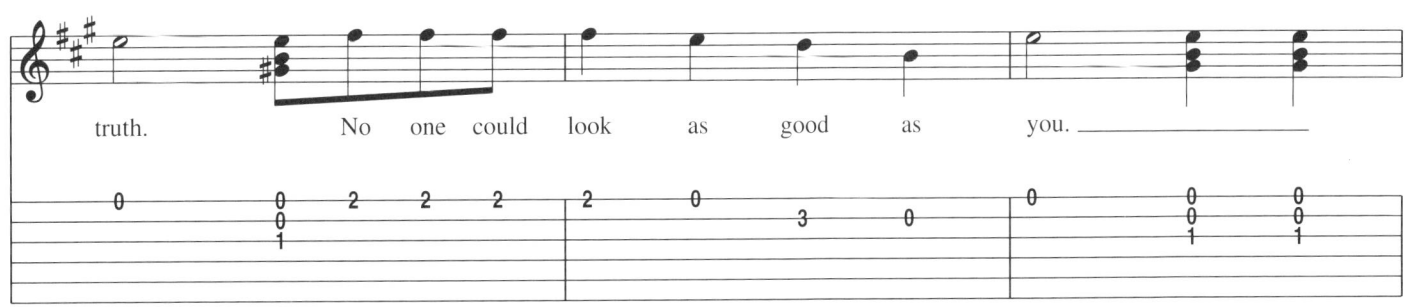

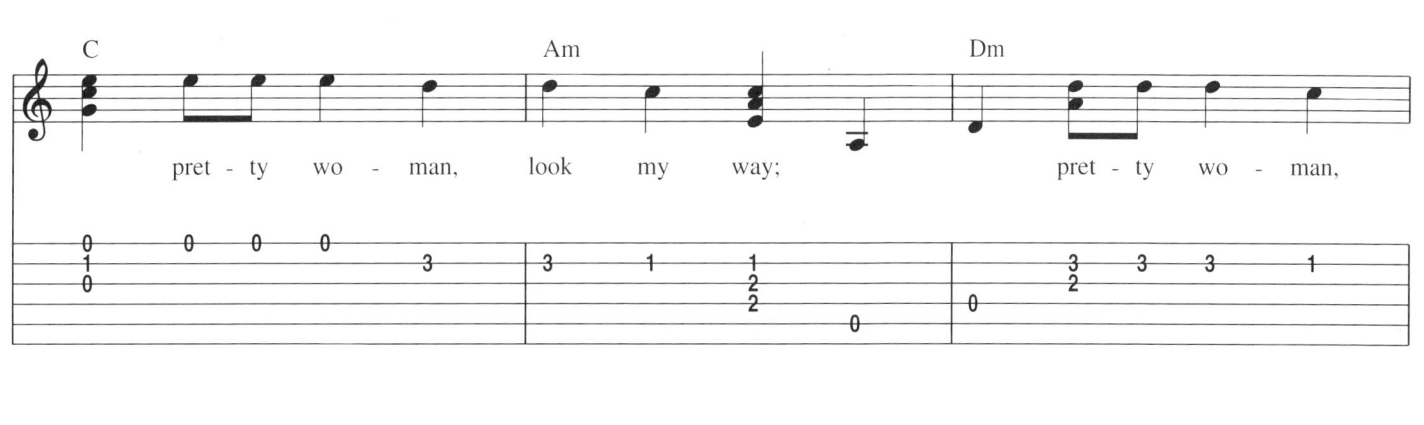

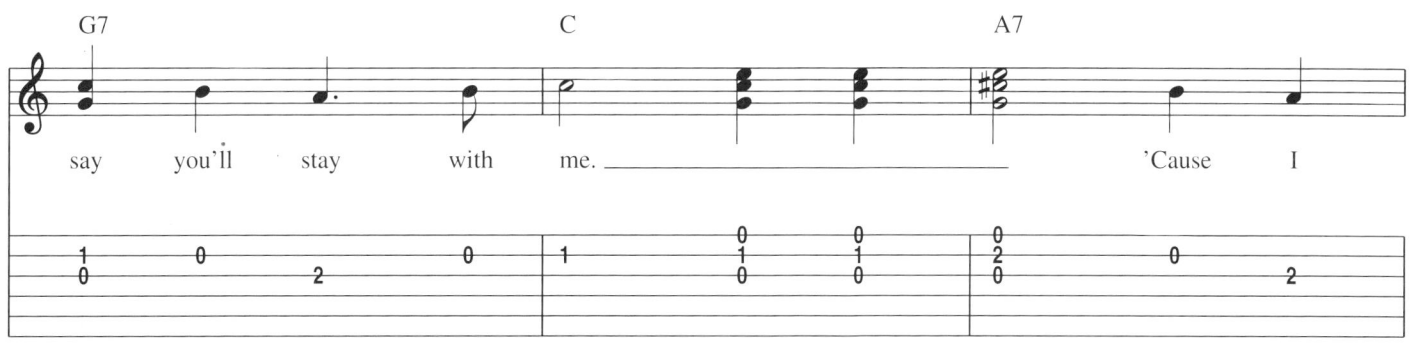

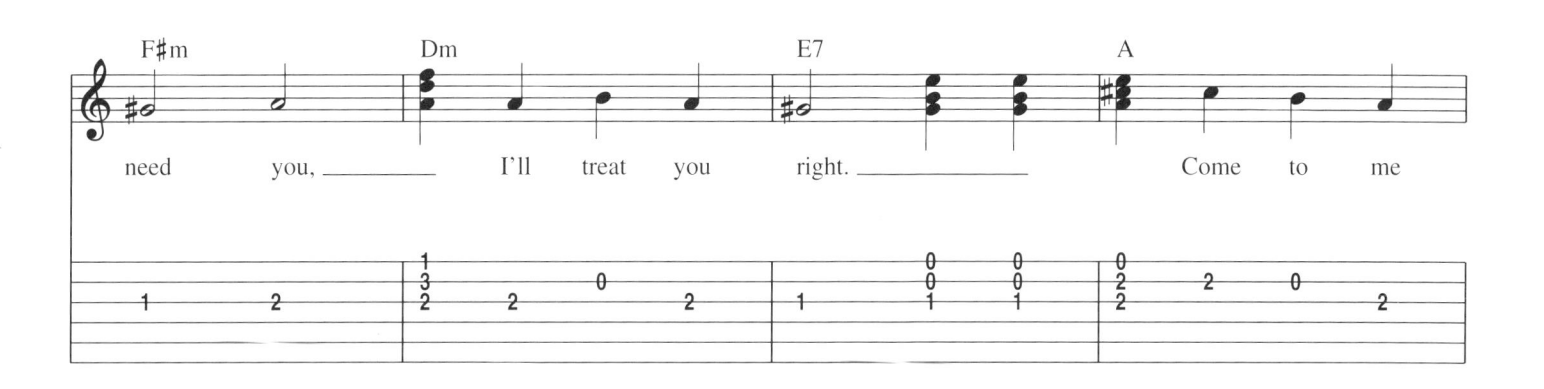

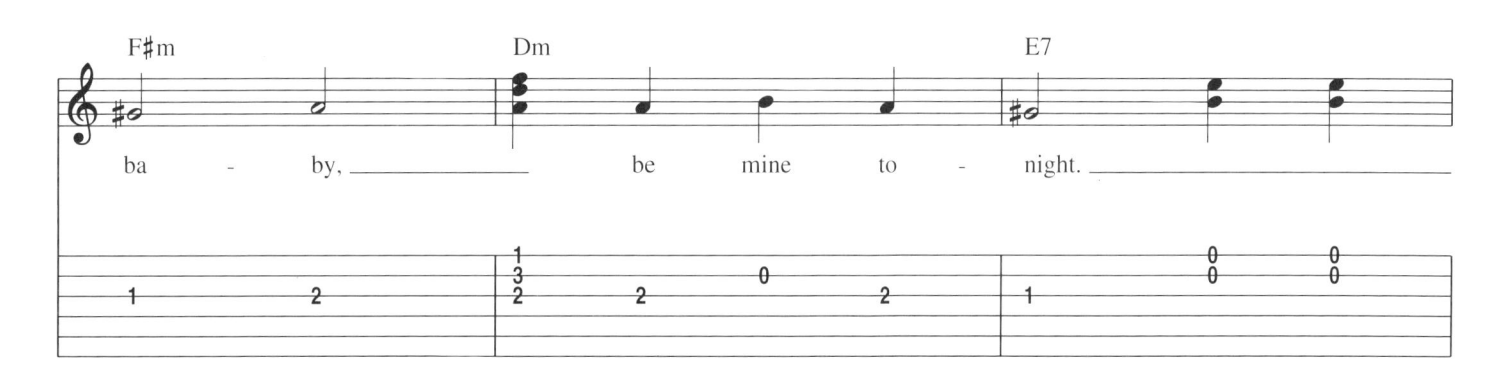

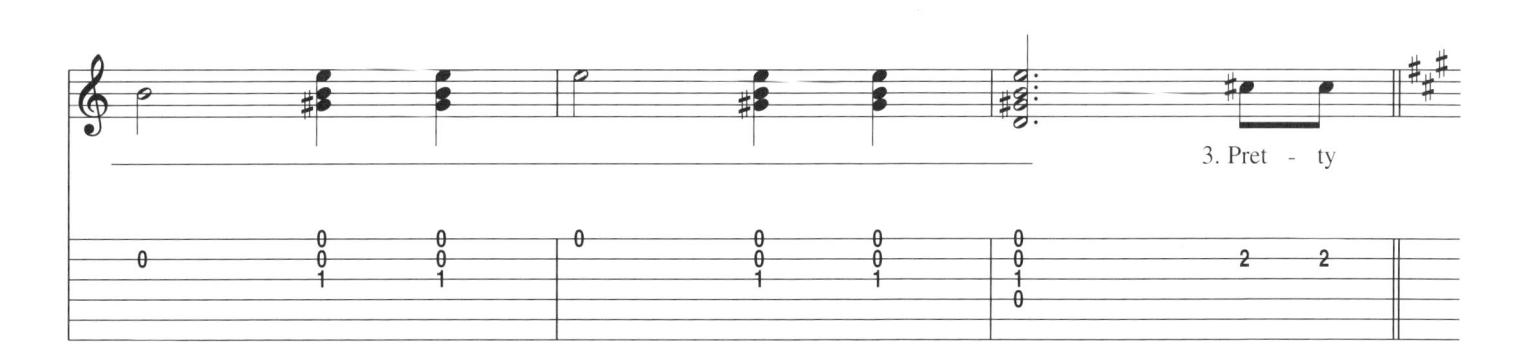

pret - ty wo - man, look my way; pret - ty wo - man, say you'll stay with me. 'Cause I need you, I'll treat you right. Come to me ba - by, be mine to - night.

3. Pret - ty

Verse

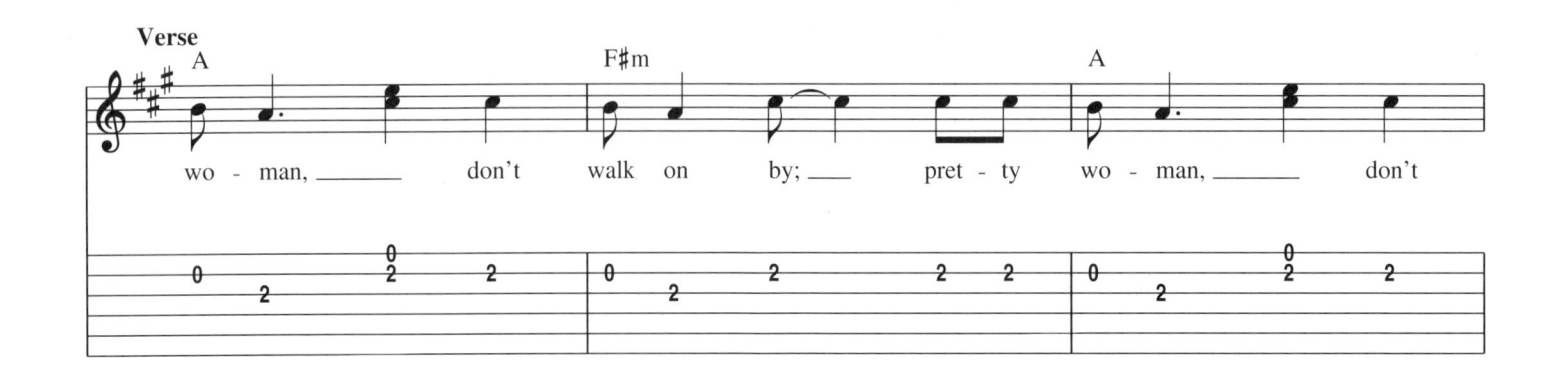

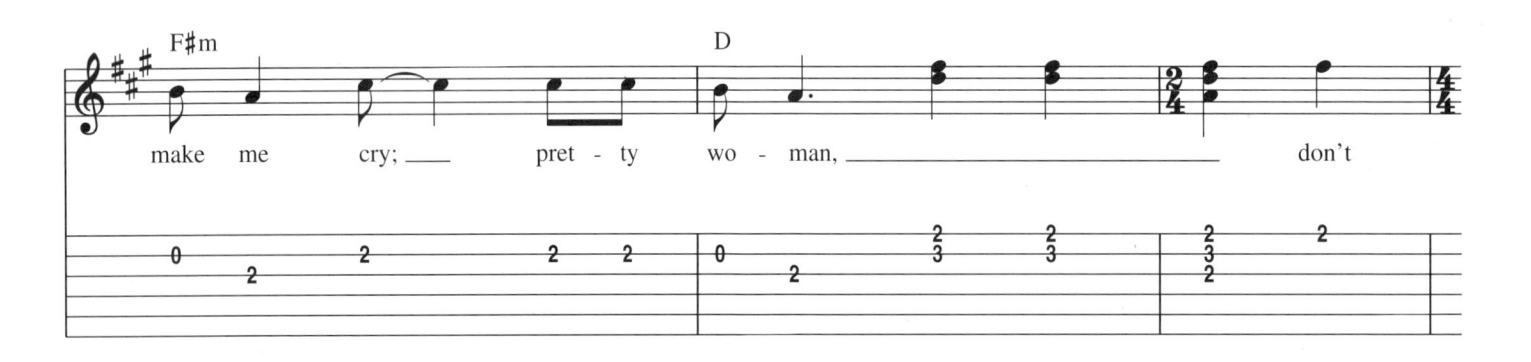

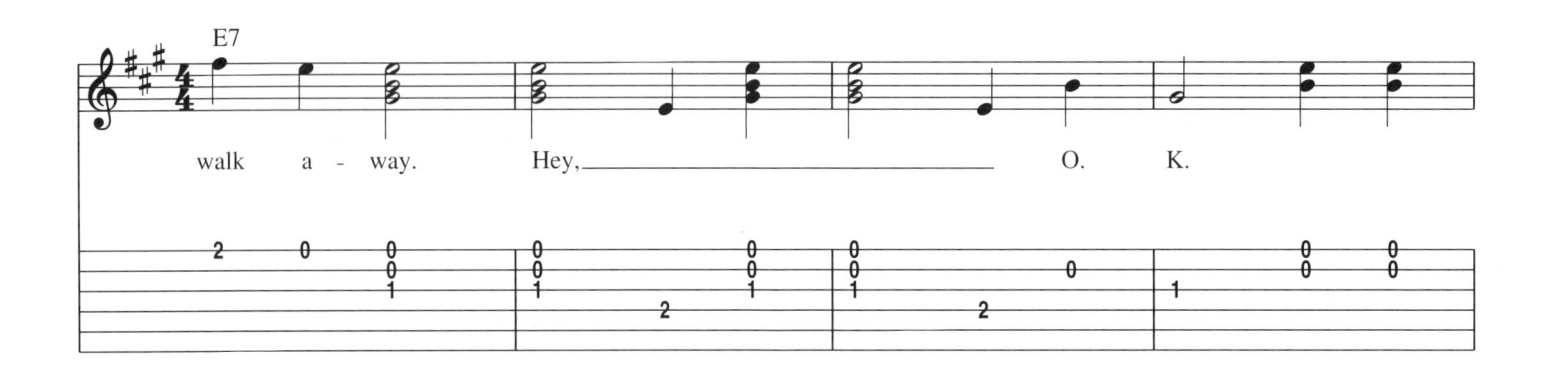

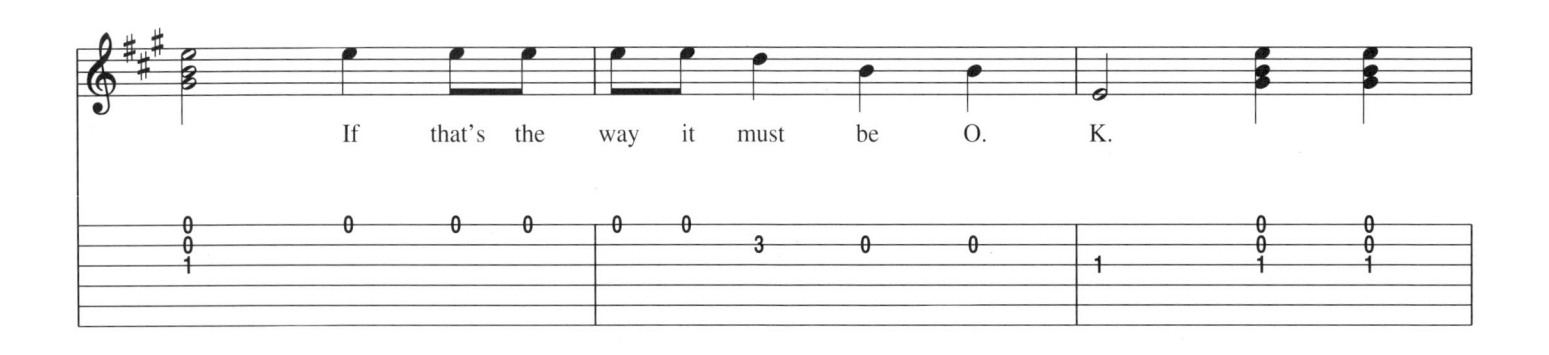

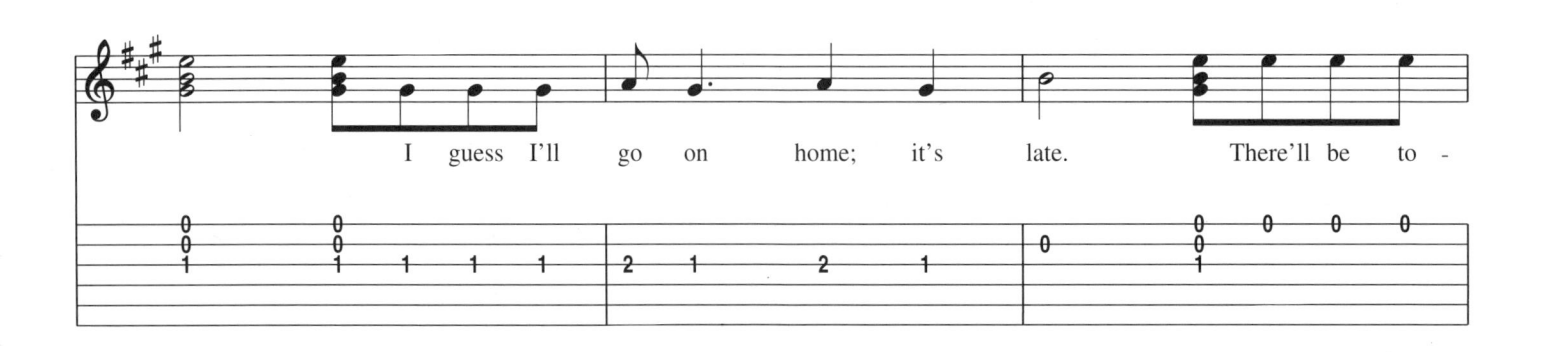

wo-man, don't walk on by; pretty wo-man, don't make me cry; pretty wo-man, don't walk a-way. Hey, O.K. If that's the way it must be O.K. I guess I'll go on home; it's late. There'll be tomor-row night but wait! What do I see? Is she walk-ing back to me? Yeah, she's walk-ing back to me! Oh, pret-ty wo-man.

Additional Lyrics

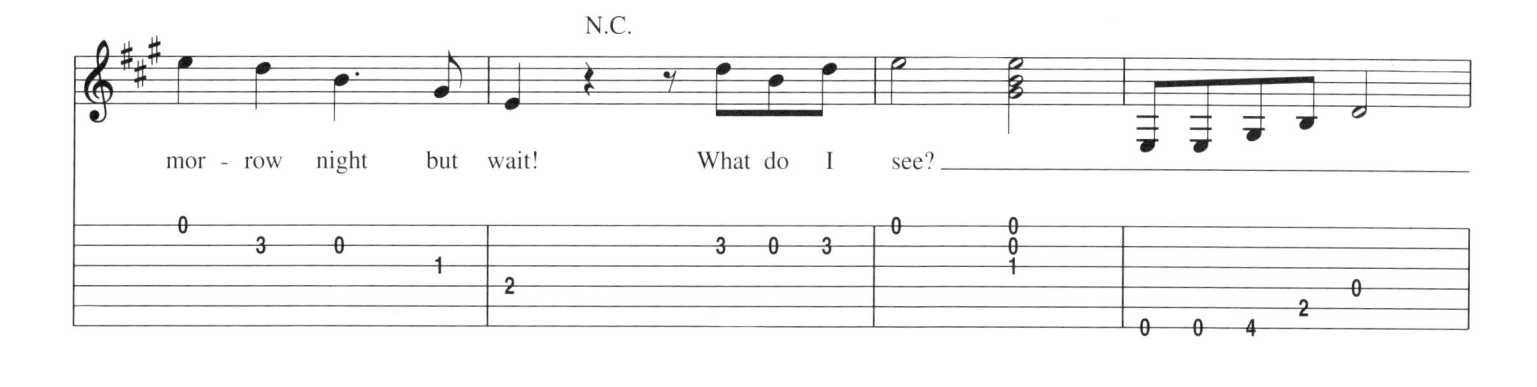

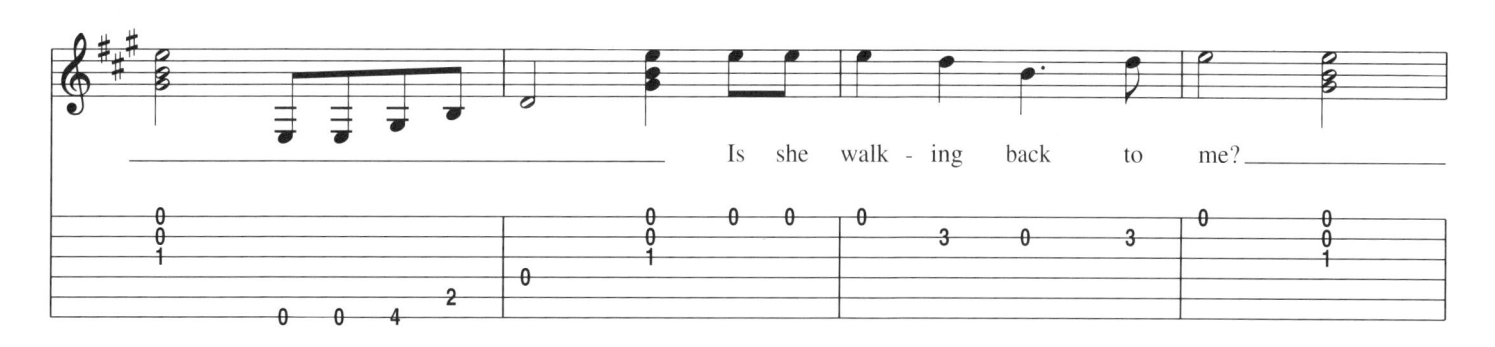

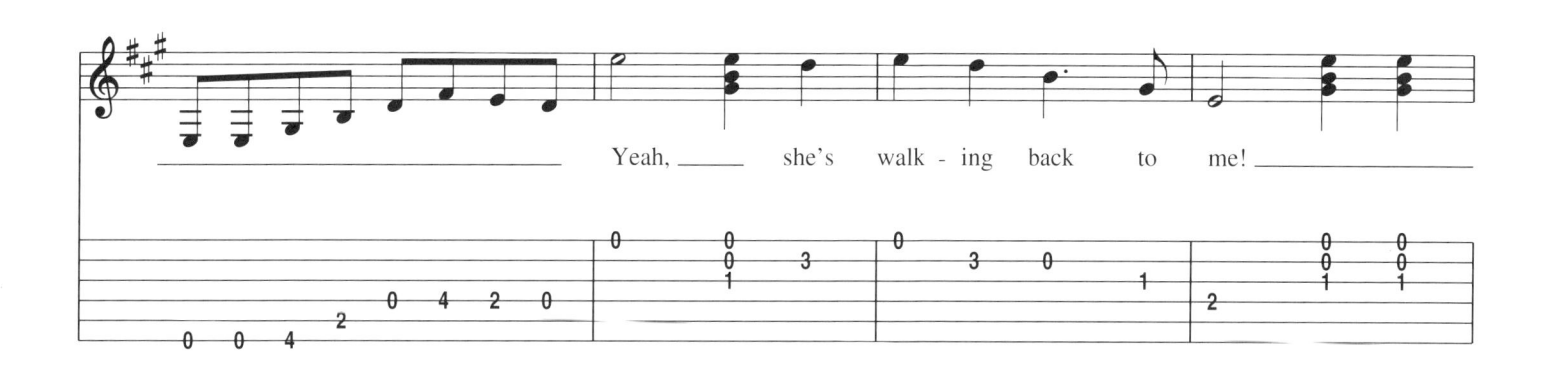

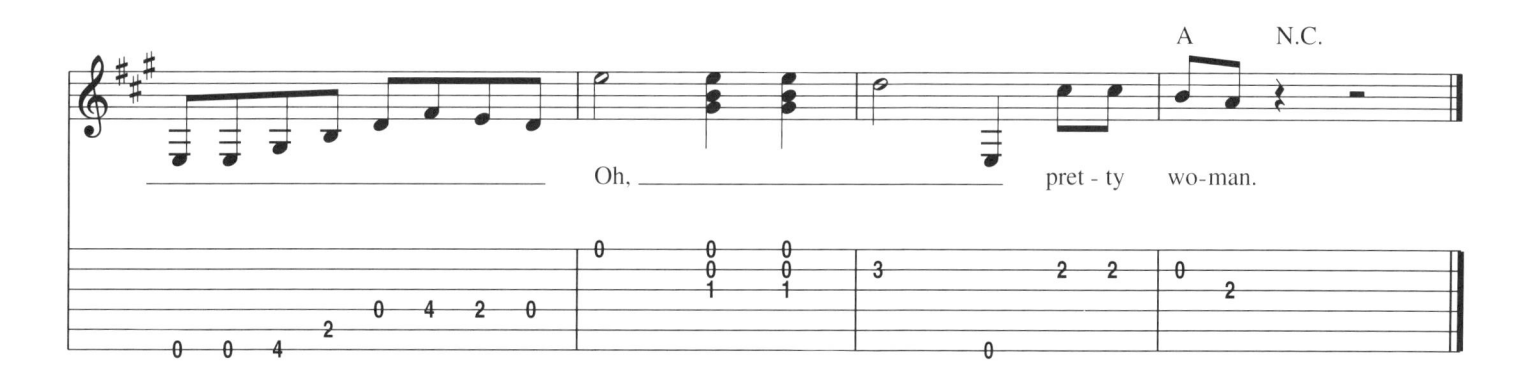

2. Pretty woman, won't you pardon me?
   Pretty woman, I couldn't help but see;
   Pretty woman, that you look lovely as can be.
   Are you lonely just like me?

Peggy Sue

Words and Music by Jerry Allison, Norman Petty and Buddy Holly

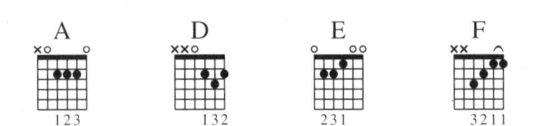

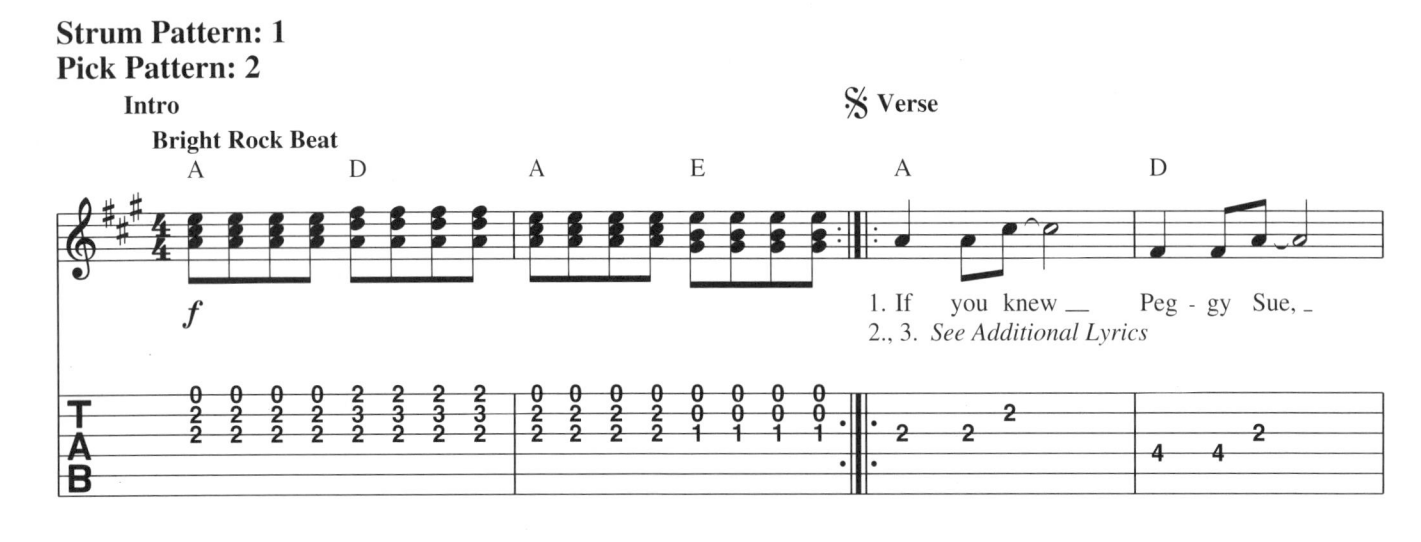

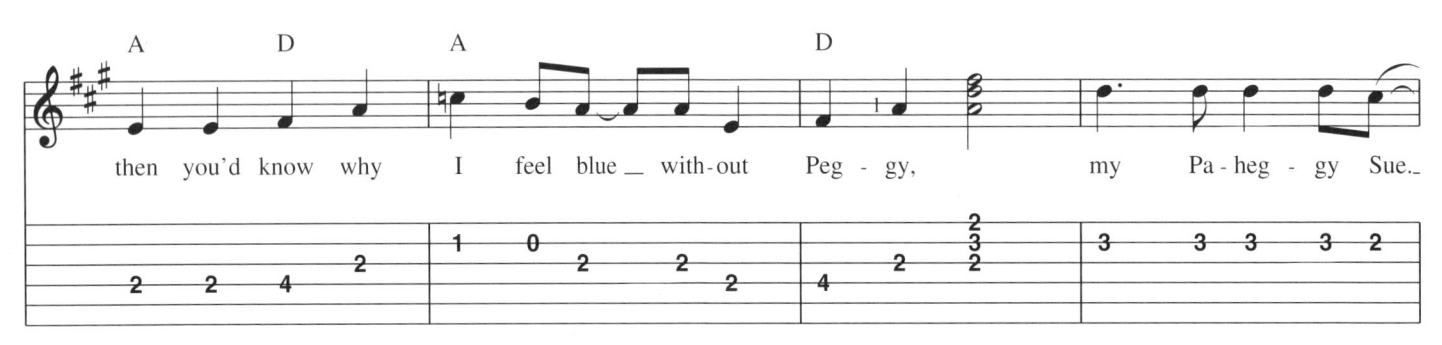

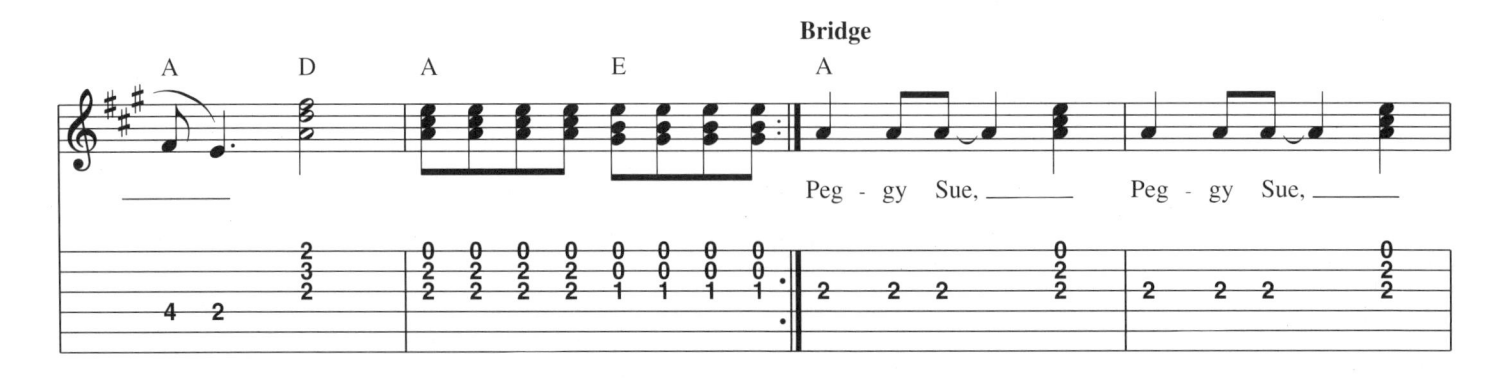

Strum Pattern: 1
Pick Pattern: 2

Intro
Bright Rock Beat

1. If you knew Peg-gy Sue,
2., 3. *See Additional Lyrics*

then you'd know why I feel blue with-out Peg-gy, my Pa-heg-gy Sue.

Oh well, I love you gal, yes I love you, Peg-gy Sue.

Bridge

Peg-gy Sue, Peg-gy Sue,

© 1957 (Renewed) MPL COMMUNICATIONS, INC. and WREN MUSIC CO.
All Rights Reserved

Additional Lyrics

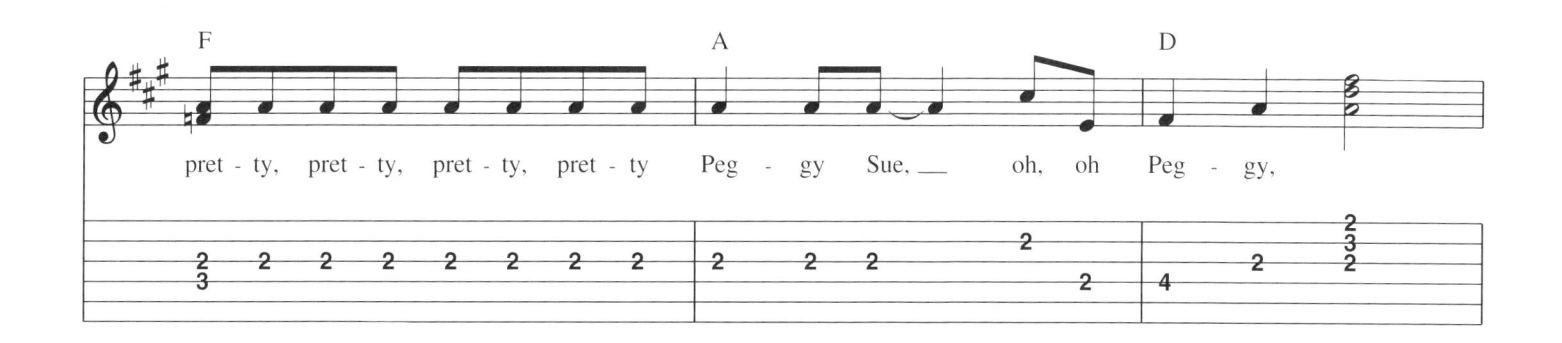

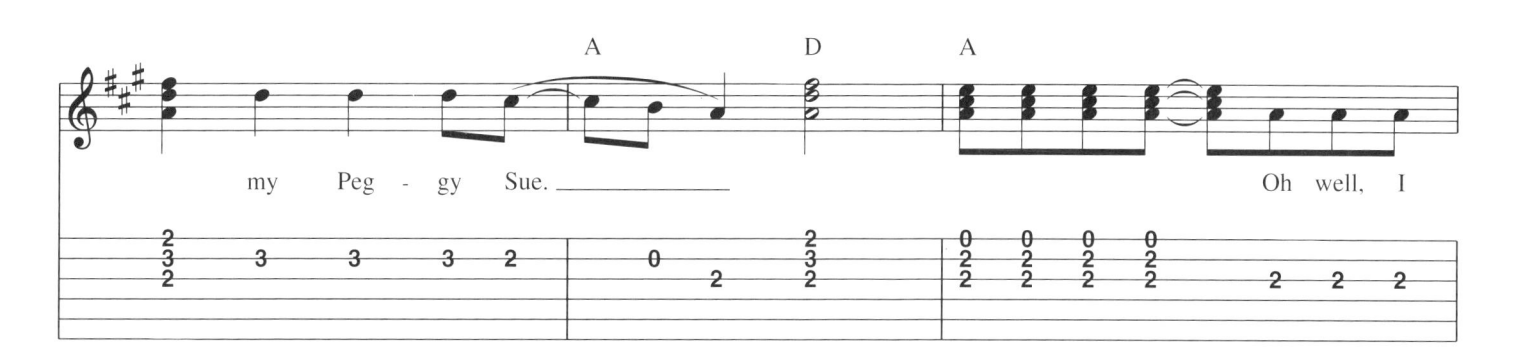

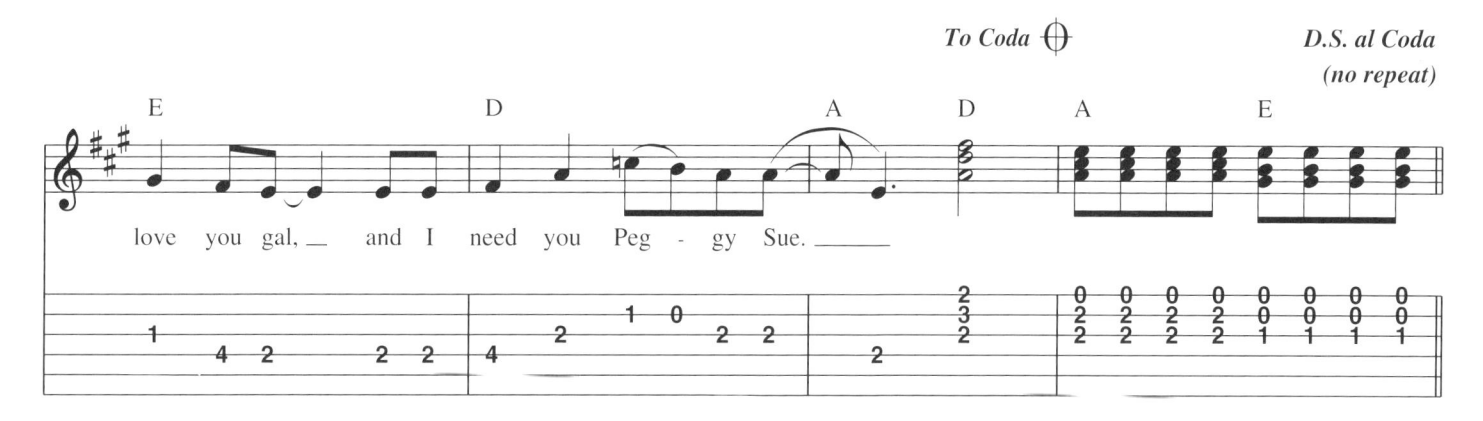

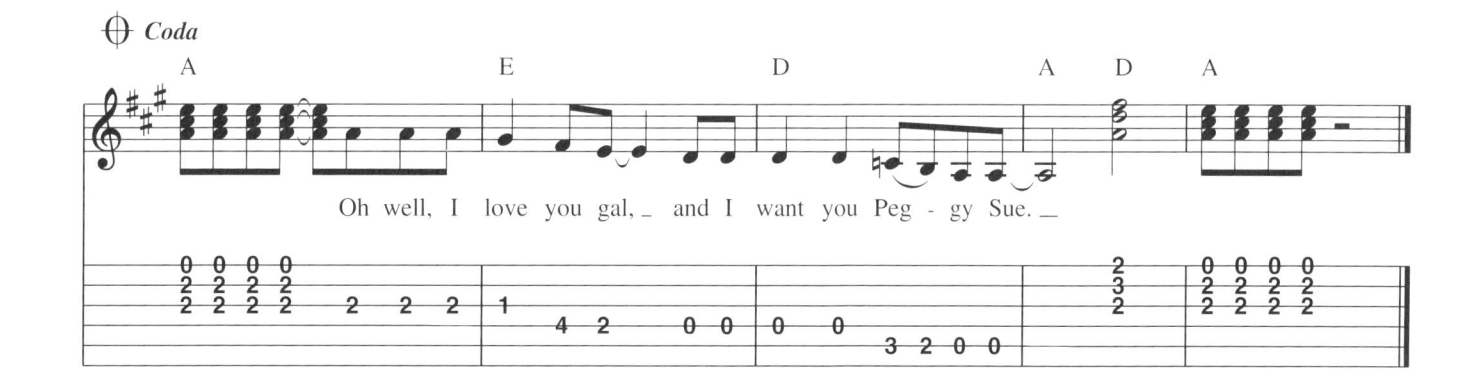

2. Peggy Sue, Peggy Sue,
   Oh how my heart yearns for you,
   Oh Peggy, my Pa-heggy Sue.
   Oh well, I love you gal, Peggy Sue.

3. I love you, Peggy Sue,
   With a love so rare and true,
   Oh Peggy, my Peggy Sue.
   Oh well, I love you gal, I want you Peggy Sue.

Rock and Roll Is Here to Stay

Words and Music by David White

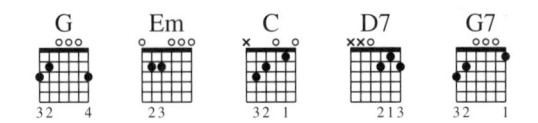

Chords: G, Em, C, D7, G7

Strum Pattern: 3
Pick Pattern: 3

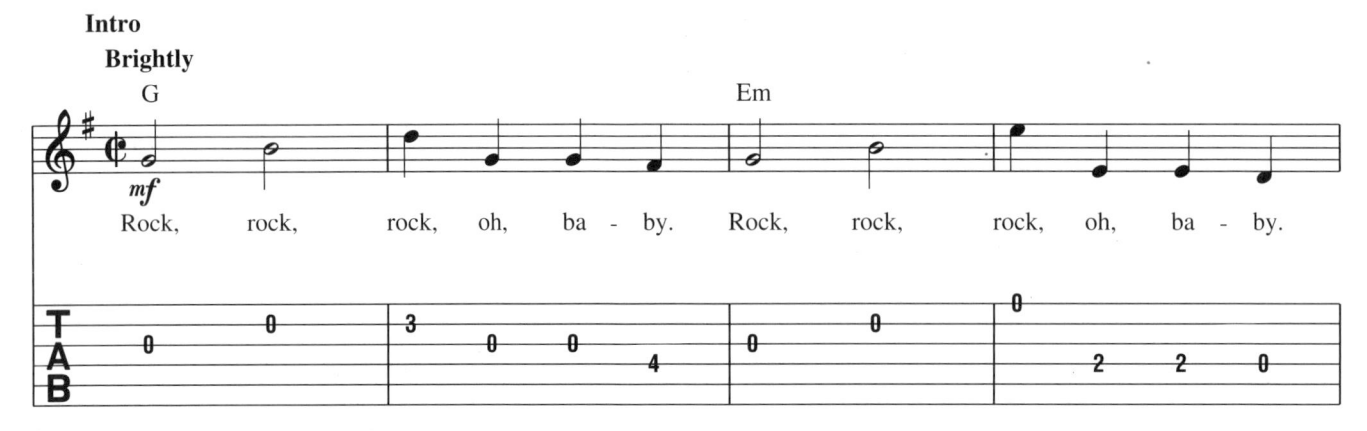

Intro
Brightly

G | | Em |

Rock, rock, rock, oh, ba - by. Rock, rock, rock, oh, ba - by.

To Coda ⊕

C | | D7 |

Rock, rock, rock, oh, ba - by. Rock, rock, rock, oh, ba - by...

Verse

G | | | G7

1. Rock and roll is here to stay, and it will nev - er die. _____
3. *See Additional Lyrics*

Copyright © 1957 (Renewed) by Arc Music Corporation (BMI) and Golden Egg Music Inc. (BMI)
International Copyright Secured   All Rights Reserved
Used by Permission

C G
It was meant to be that way, though I don't know why.
D C G
I don't care what peo - ple say, rock and roll is here to stay!
D C G
We don't care what peo-ple say, rock and roll is here to stay.
Verse
G G7
2., 4. Rock and roll will al - ways be, I dig it to the end.
C G
It 'll go down in his - to - ry, just you watch my friend.

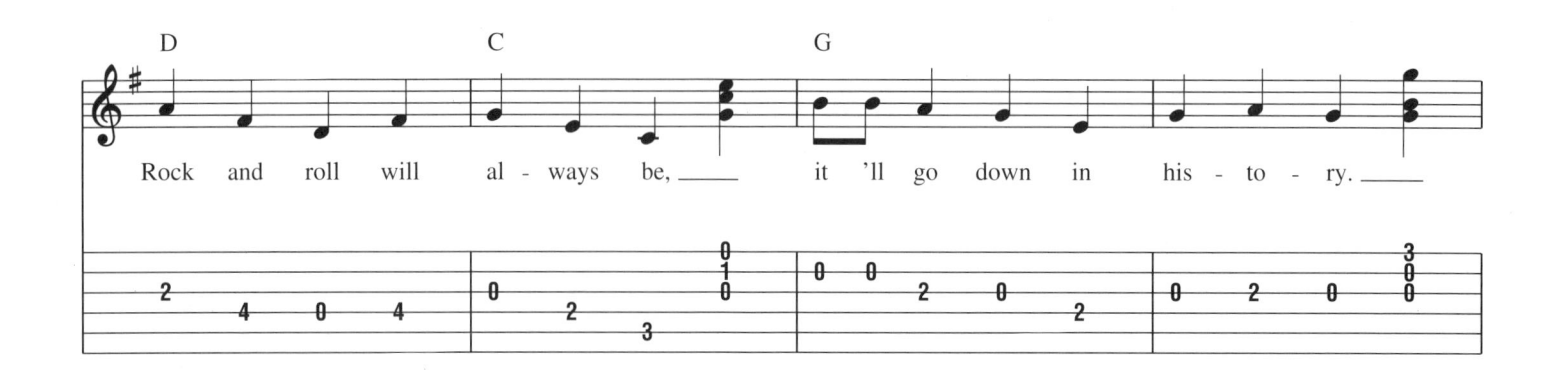

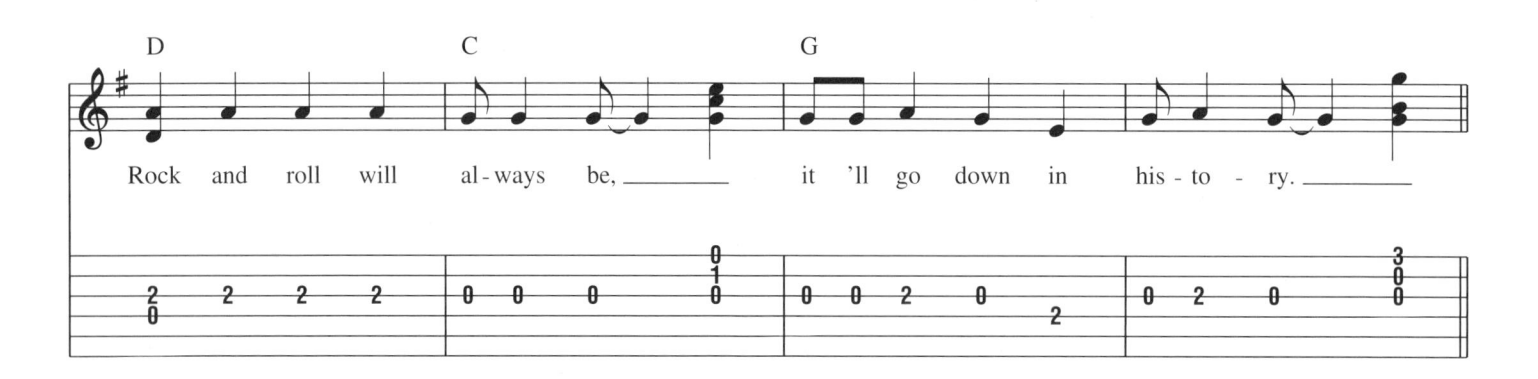

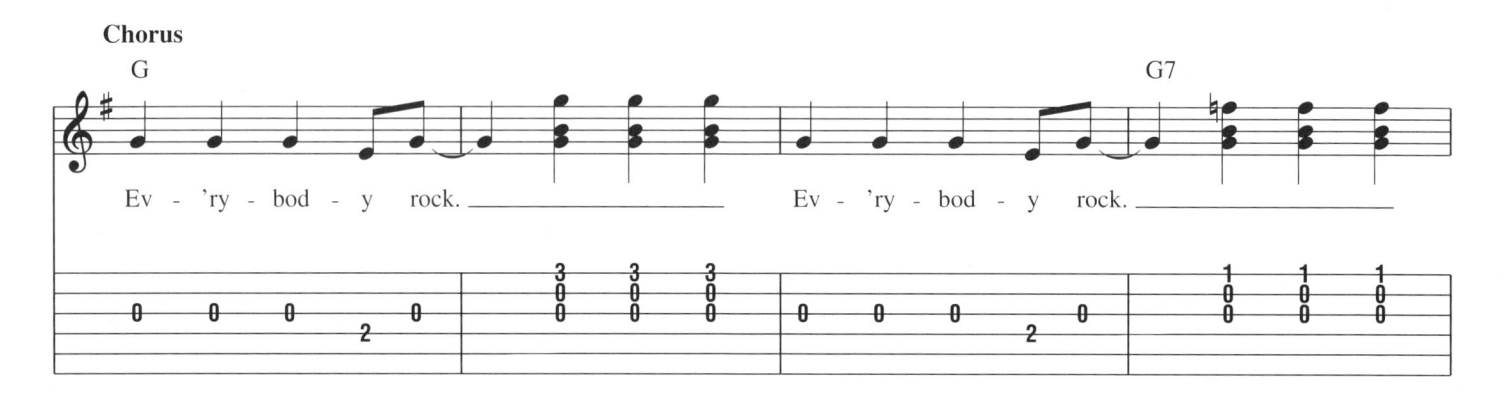

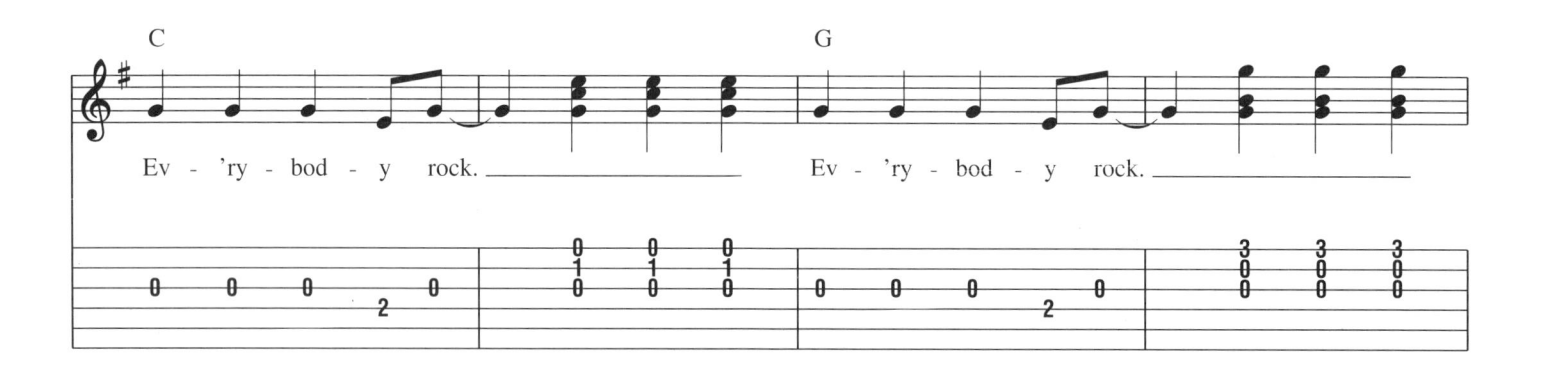

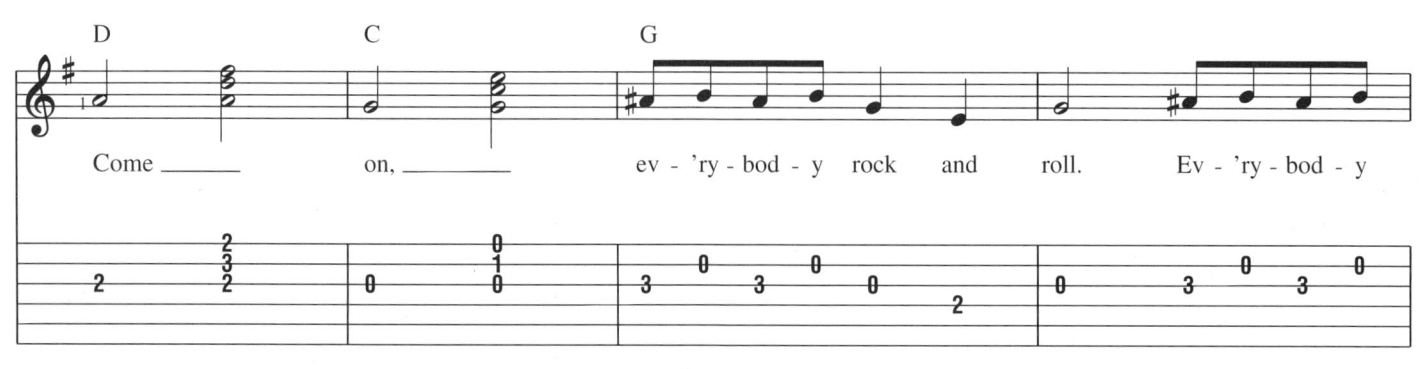

Rock and roll will always be, ___ it'll go down in his-to-ry. ___

Rock and roll will always be, ___ it'll go down in his-to-ry. ___

Chorus

Ev-'ry-bod-y rock. ___ Ev-'ry-bod-y rock. ___

Ev-'ry-bod-y rock. ___ Ev-'ry-bod-y rock. ___

Come ___ on, ___ ev-'ry-bod-y rock and roll. Ev-'ry-bod-y

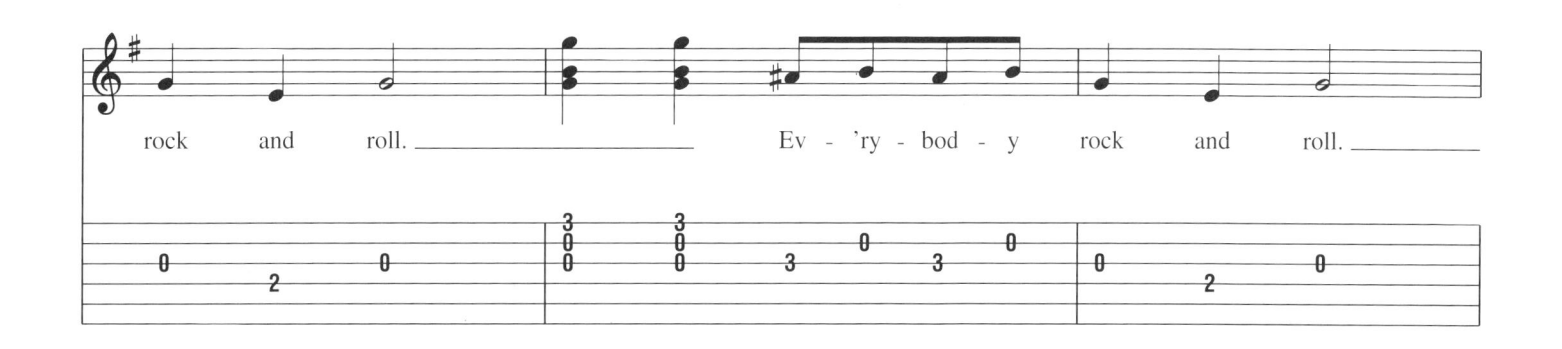

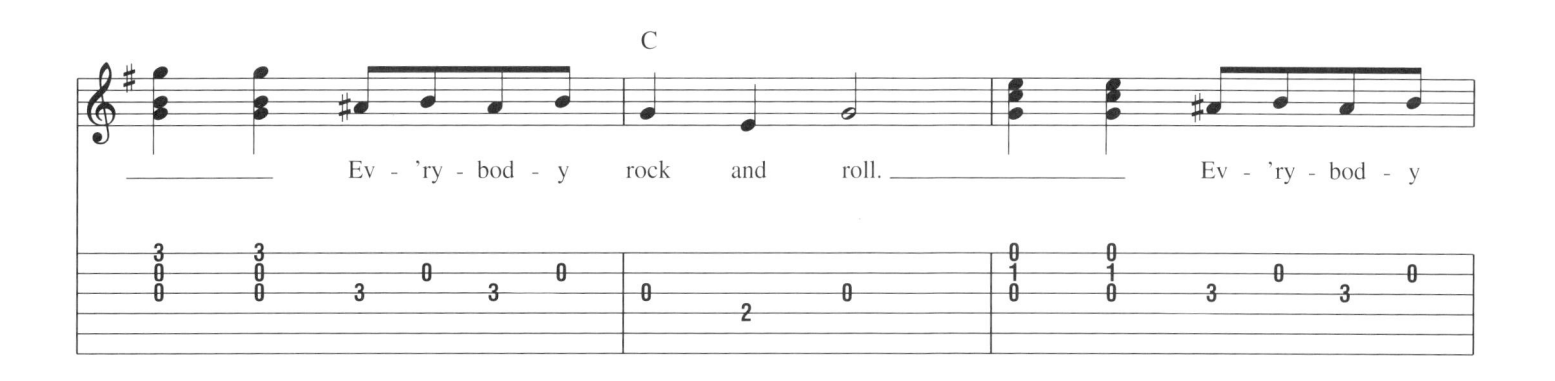

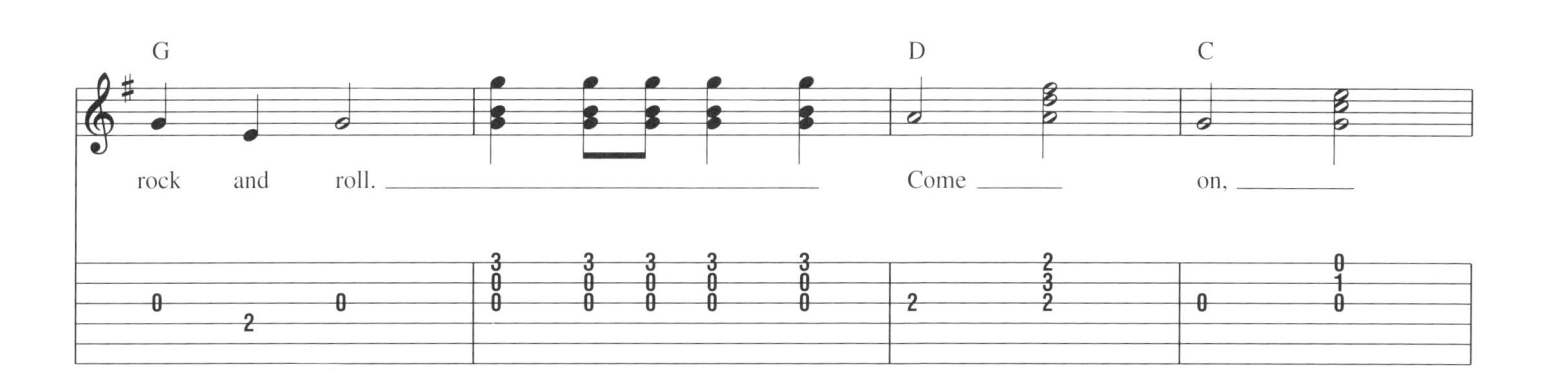

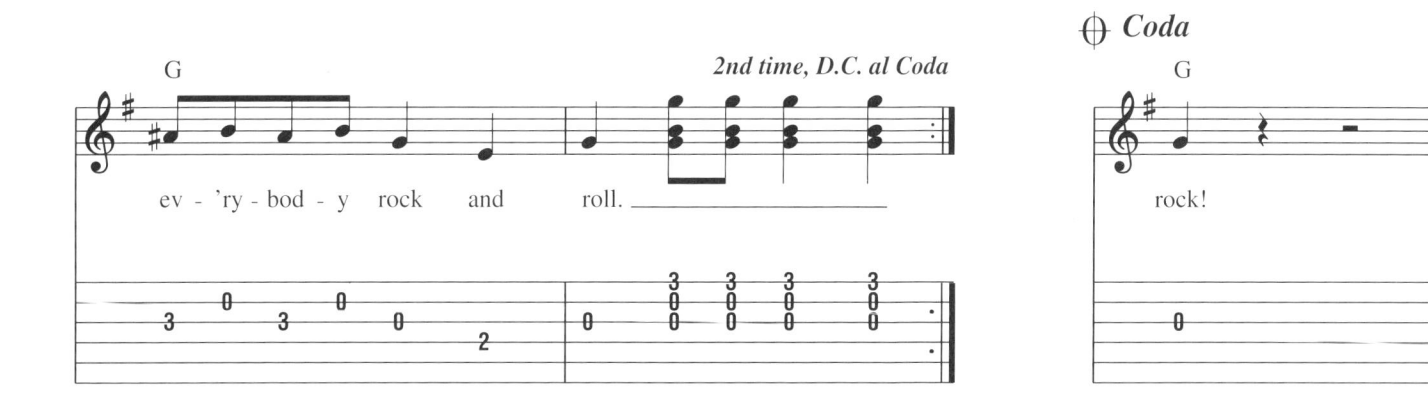

Additional Lyrics

3. If you don't like rock and roll, just think what you've been missin'.
   But if you like to bop and stroll, walk around and listen.
   Let's all start to rock and roll, ev'rybody rock and roll.

Rock Around the Clock

Words and Music by Max C. Freedman and Jimmy DeKnight

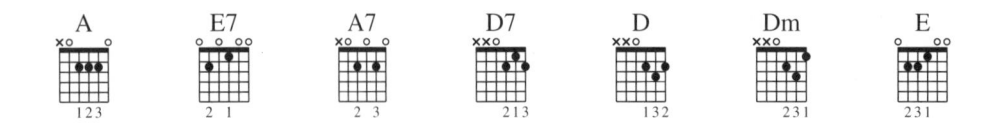

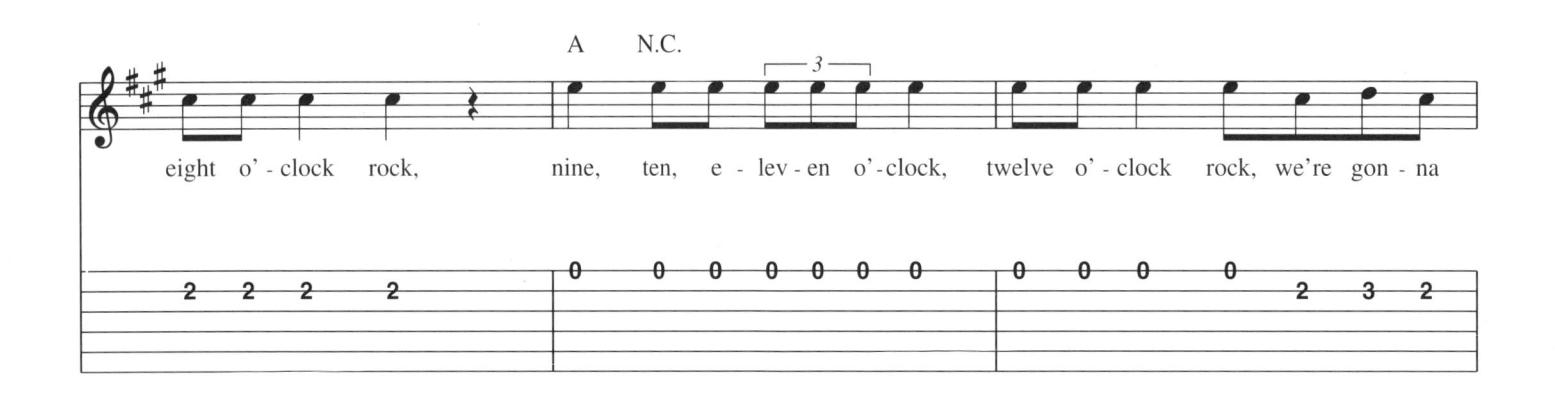

Chords: A, E7, A7, D7, D, Dm, E

Strum Pattern: 1
Pick Pattern: 2

Intro
Bright Shuffle

One, two, three o'-clock, four o'-clock rock, five, six, sev-en o'-clock, eight o'-clock rock, nine, ten, e-lev-en o'-clock, twelve o'-clock rock, we're gon-na rock a-round the clock to-night._ 1. Put your glad rags on and join me, Hon._ We'll
2., 3., 4., 5. *See Additional Lyrics*

Copyright © 1953 by Myers Music, Inc.
Copyright Renewed 1981 by Myers Music, Inc. and Capano Music
International Copyright Secured   All Rights Reserved

Lyrics under staves:

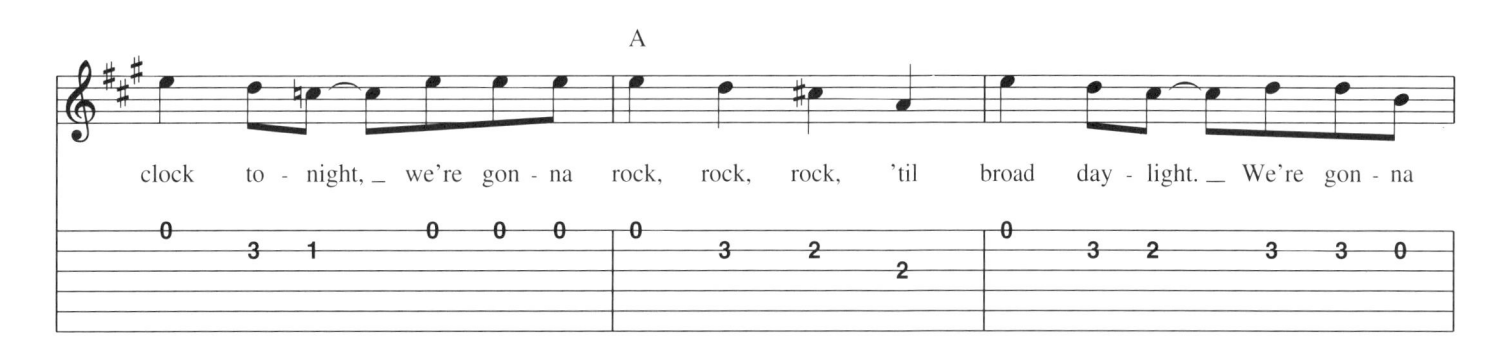

have some fun when the clock strikes one.__ We're gon-na rock a-round the clock to-night,__ we're gon-na rock, rock, rock, 'til broad day-light.__ We're gon-na rock, gon-na rock a-round__ the clock__ to-night._____ 2. When the

Additional Lyrics

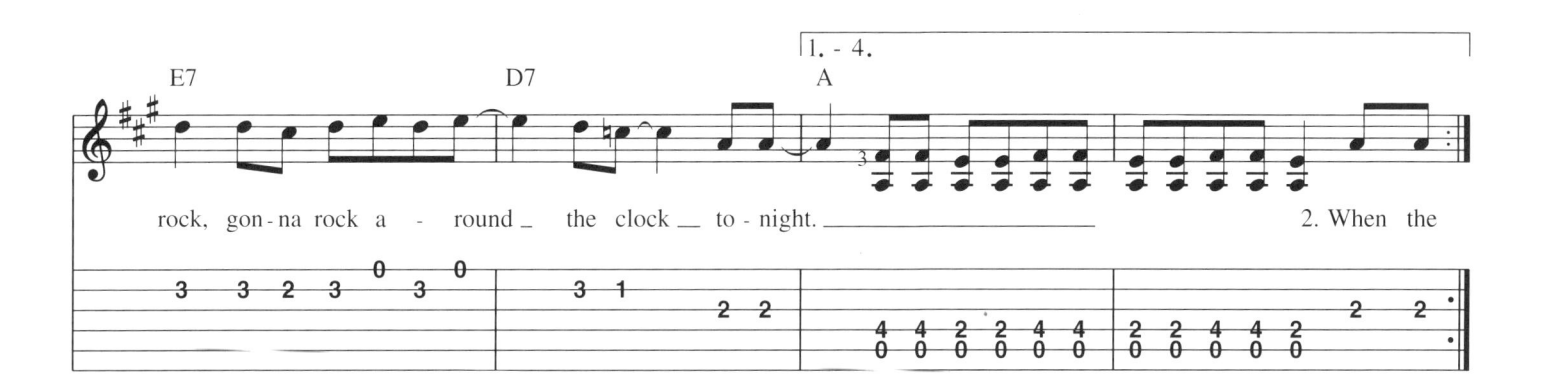

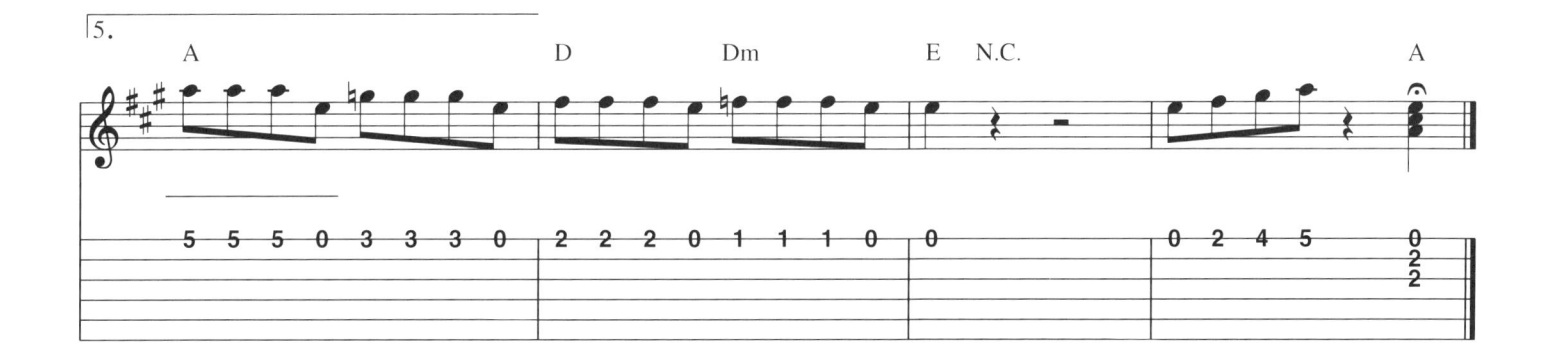

2. When the clock strikes two, and three and four,
   If the band slows down we'll yell for more.
   We're gonna rock around the clock tonight,
   We're gonna rock, rock, rock, 'til broad daylight.
   We're gonna rock, gonna rock around the clock tonight.

3. When the chimes ring five and six and seven,
   We'll be rockin' up in seventh heav'n.
   We're gonna rock around the clock tonight,
   We're gonna rock, rock, rock, 'til broad daylight.
   We're gonna rock, gonna rock around the clock tonight.

4. When it's eight, nine, ten, eleven, too,
   I'll be goin' strong and so will you.
   We're gonna rock around the clock tonight,
   We're gonna rock, rock, rock, 'til broad daylight.
   We're gonna rock, gonna rock around the clock tonight.

5. When the clock strikes twelve, we'll cool off, then,
   Start a rockin' 'round the clock again.
   We're gonna rock around the clock tonight,
   We're gonna rock, rock, rock, 'til broad daylight.
   We're gonna rock, gonna rock around the clock tonight.

Searchin'

Words and Music by Jerry Leiber and Mike Stoller

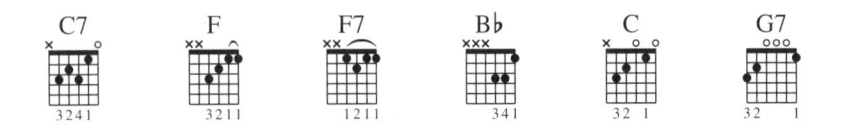

Chords: C7, F, F7, Bb, C, G7

Strum Pattern: 4
Pick Pattern: 1

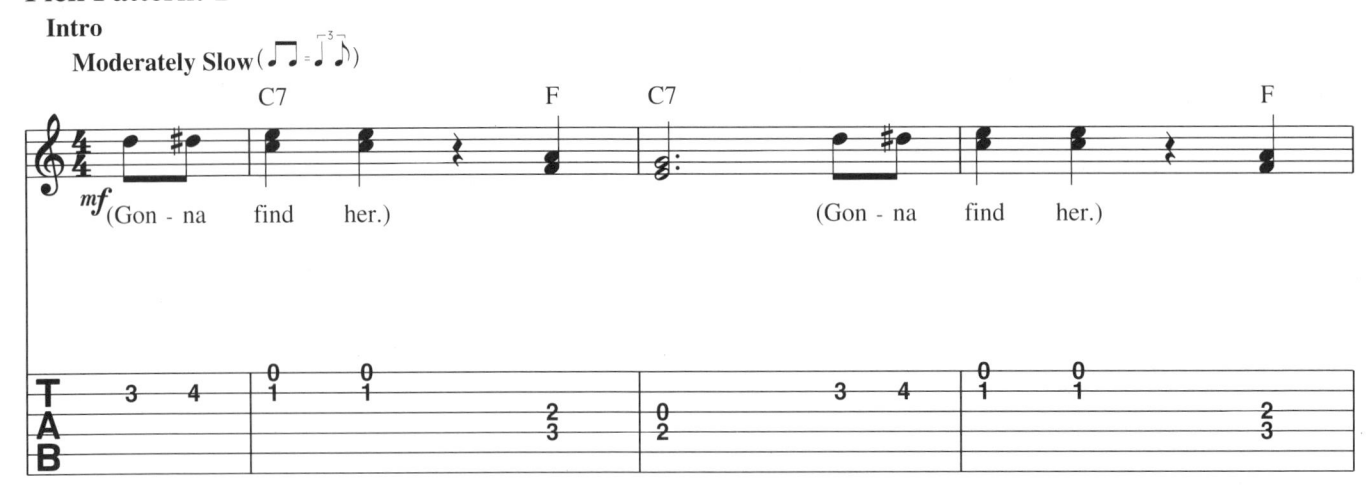

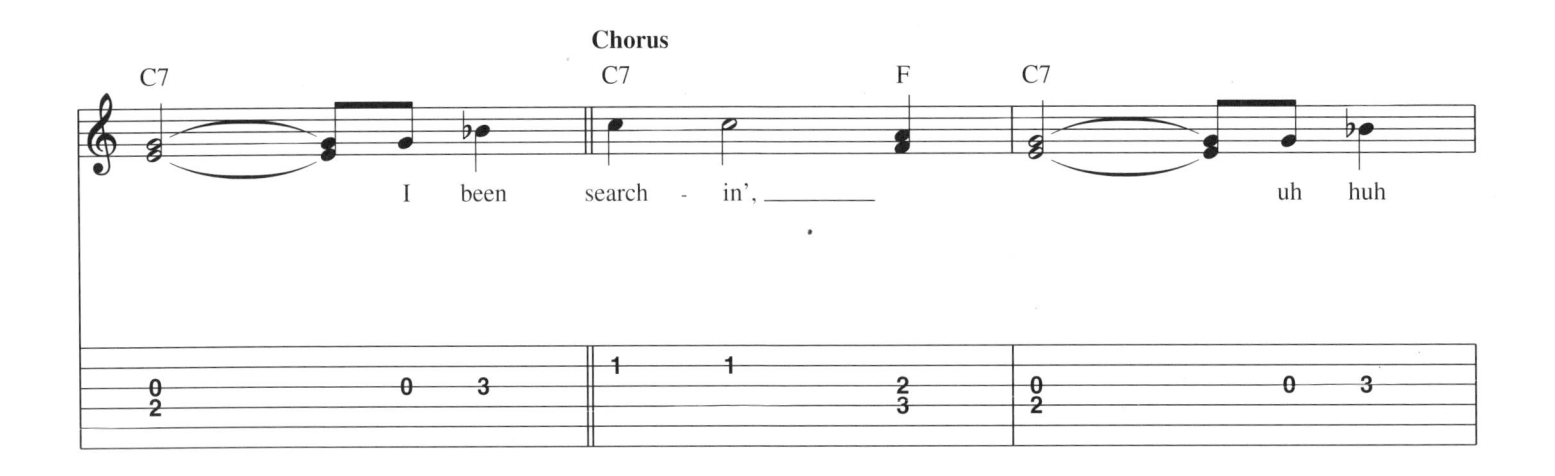

Intro
Moderately Slow ($\sqrt{}$ = $\sqrt[3]{}$)

(Gon-na find her.) (Gon-na find her.)

Chorus

I been search-in', _____ uh huh search-in', _____ oh yeah, search-in' ev-'ry

© 1957 (Renewed) JERRY LEIBER MUSIC, MIKE STOLLER MUSIC and CHAPPELL & CO.
All Rights Reserved

C7 F C7 C7
which a - way. Oh yeah, I been
F7 B♭ F7 B♭
search - in', search - in',
F7 C7 F C7 F
search - in' ev - 'ry which a -
C7 C G7
way. I'm like that North - west
F7 N.C.
Mount - ie, you know I'll bring her in some

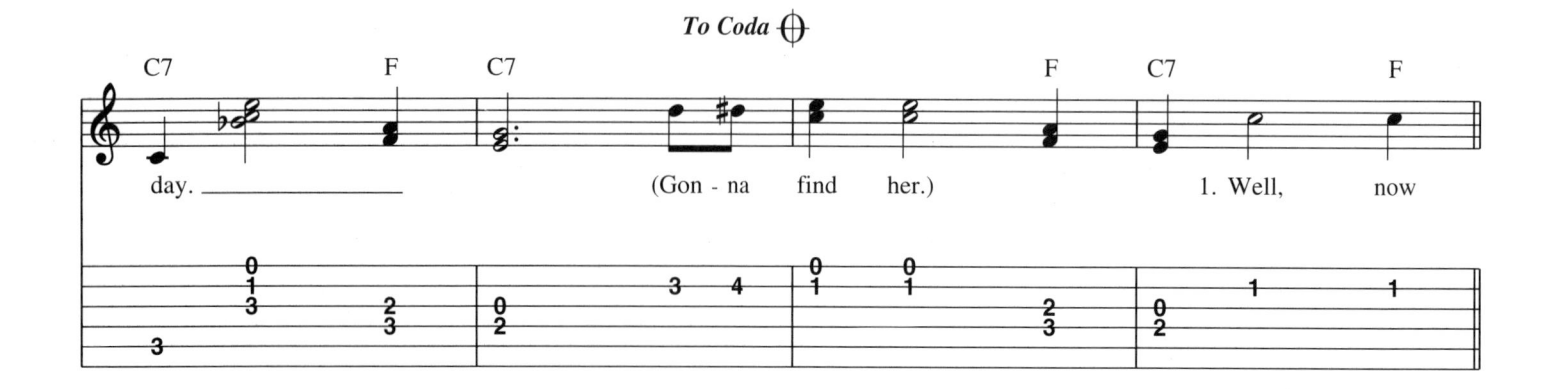

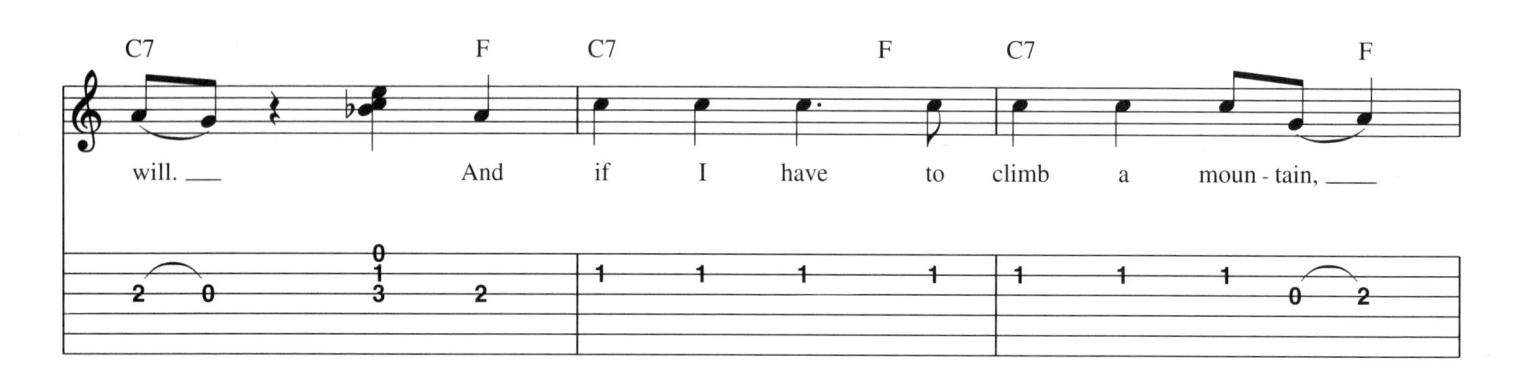

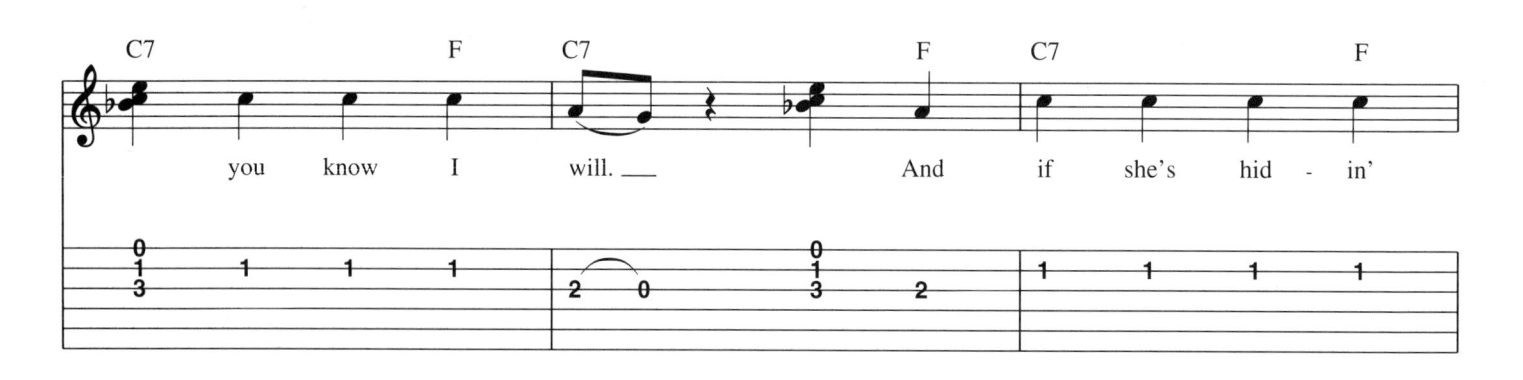

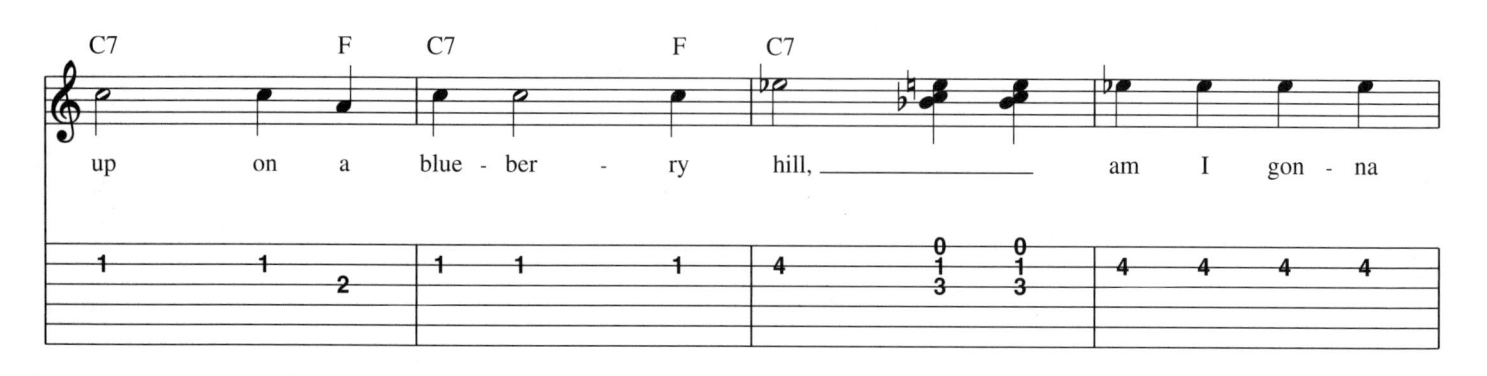

To Coda

day. _____ (Gon - na find her.) 1. Well, now

Verse

if I have to swim a riv - er, you know I
2. *See Additional Lyrics*

will. ___ And if I have to climb a moun - tain, ___

you know I will. ___ And if she's hid - in'

up on a blue - ber - ry hill, _____ am I gon - na

Additional Lyrics

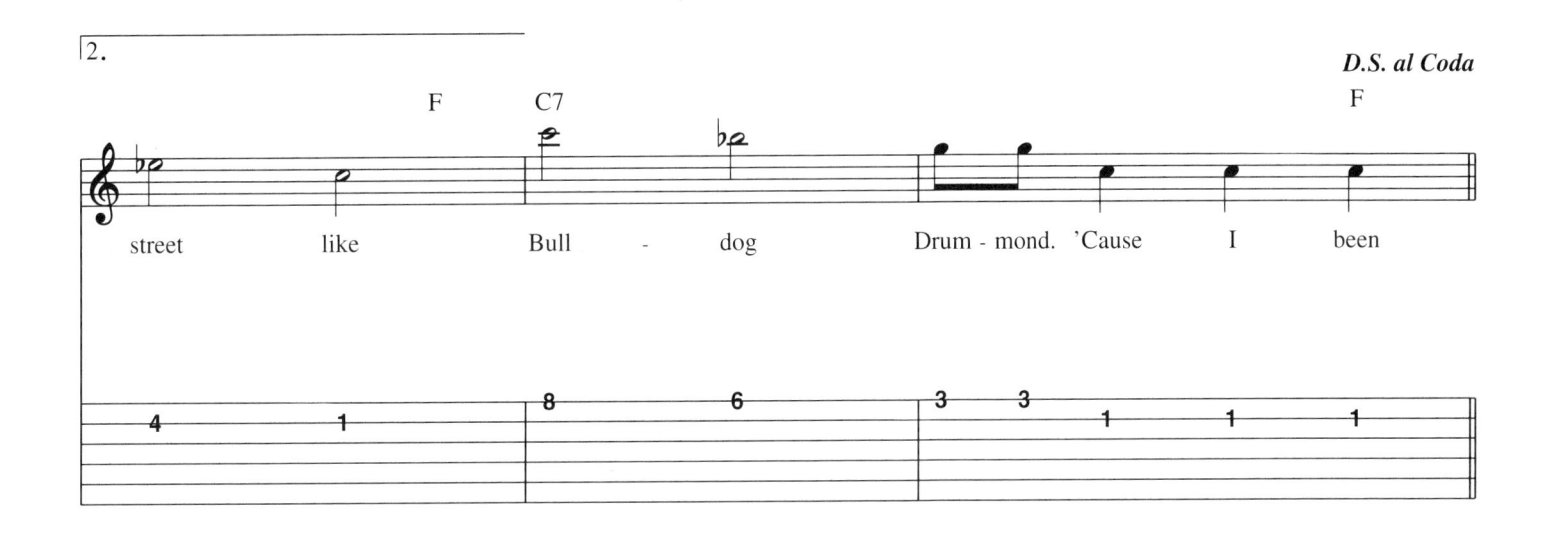

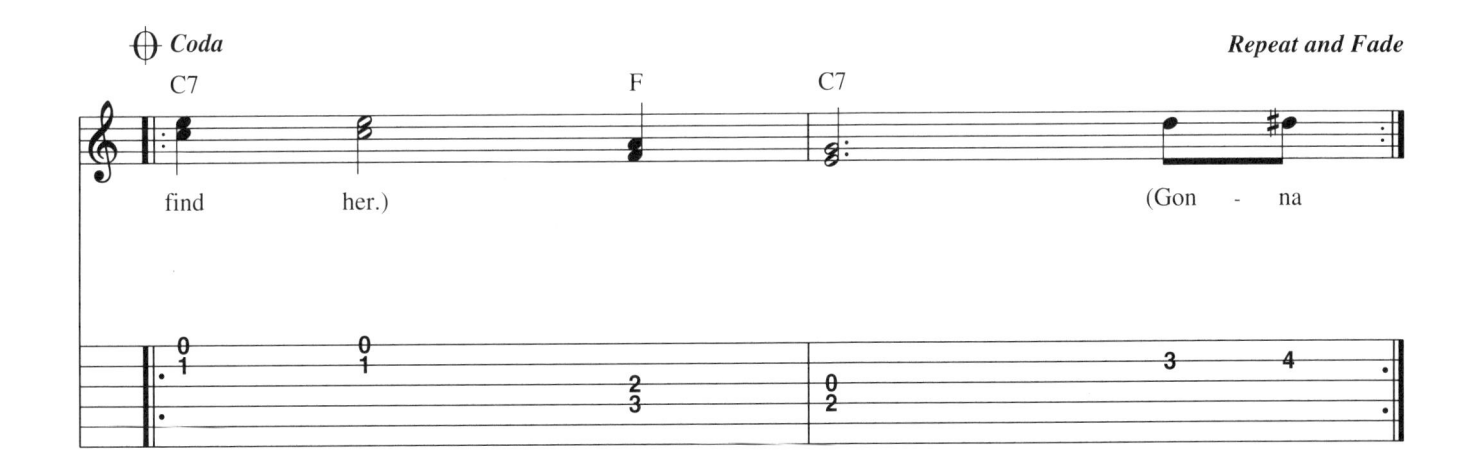

2. Well, now Sherlock Holmes, Sam Spade, got nothin', child, on me,
   Sergeant Friday, Charlie Chan and Boston Blackie.
   No matter where she's hidin', she's gonna hear me comin'.
   I'm gonna walk right down that street like Bulldog Drummond.

Shake, Rattle and Roll

Words and Music by Charles Calhoun

Chords: C, C7, F, G7, F7

Strum Pattern: 3
Pick Pattern: 3

Verse
Moderately

1. Get out from that kitch-en and rat-tle those pots and pans.
2., 3., 4. *See Additional Lyrics*

Get out from that kitch-en and rat-tle those pots and pans;

well, roll my break-fast, 'cause I'm a hun-gry man.

Copyright © 1954 by Unichappell Music Inc.
Copyright Renewed
International Copyright Secured   All Rights Reserved

Chorus

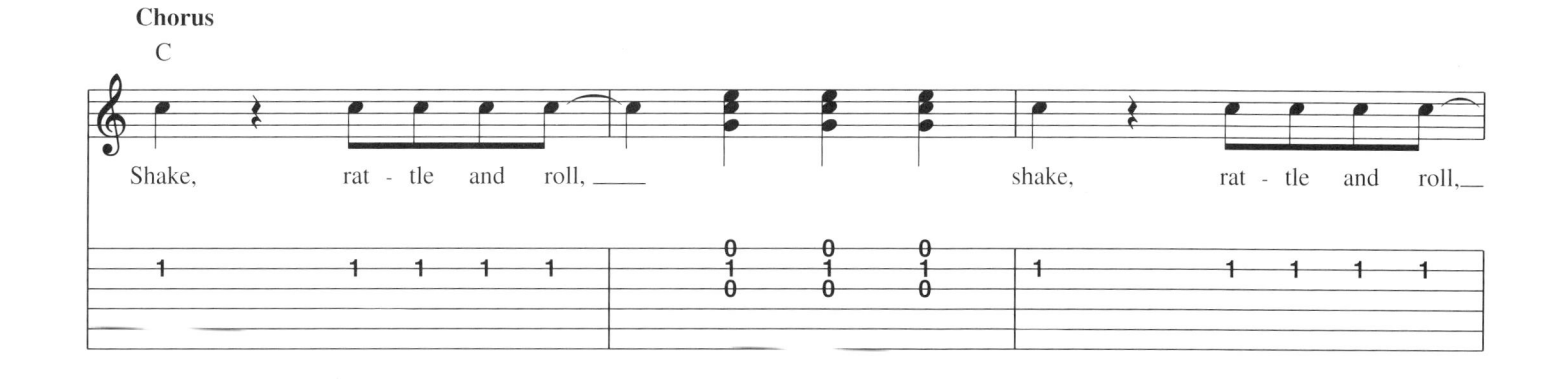

Shake, rat-tle and roll, ___ shake, rat-tle and roll, ___ shake, rat-tle and roll, ___ you nev-er do noth-in' to save your dog-gone soul. ___ soul. ___

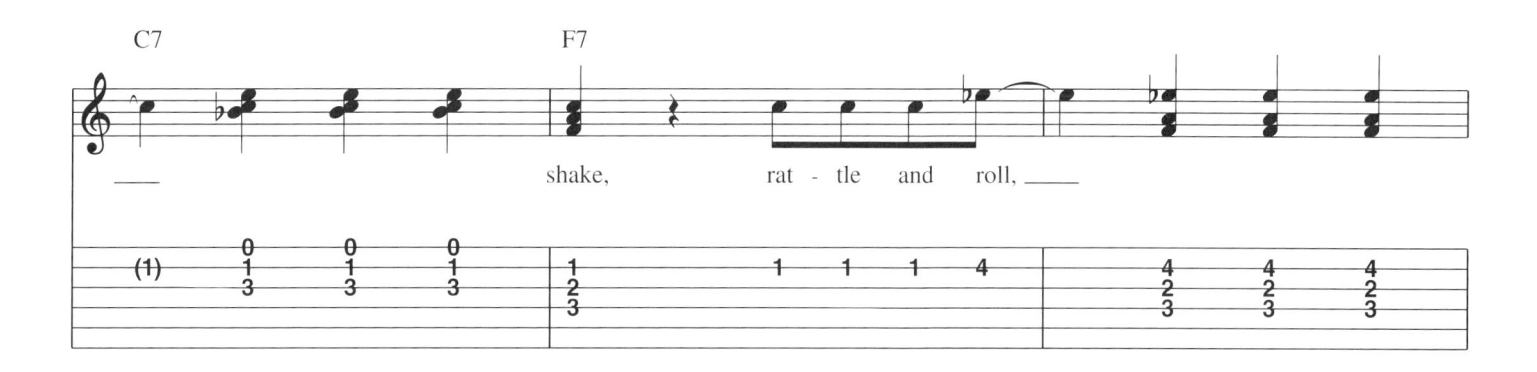

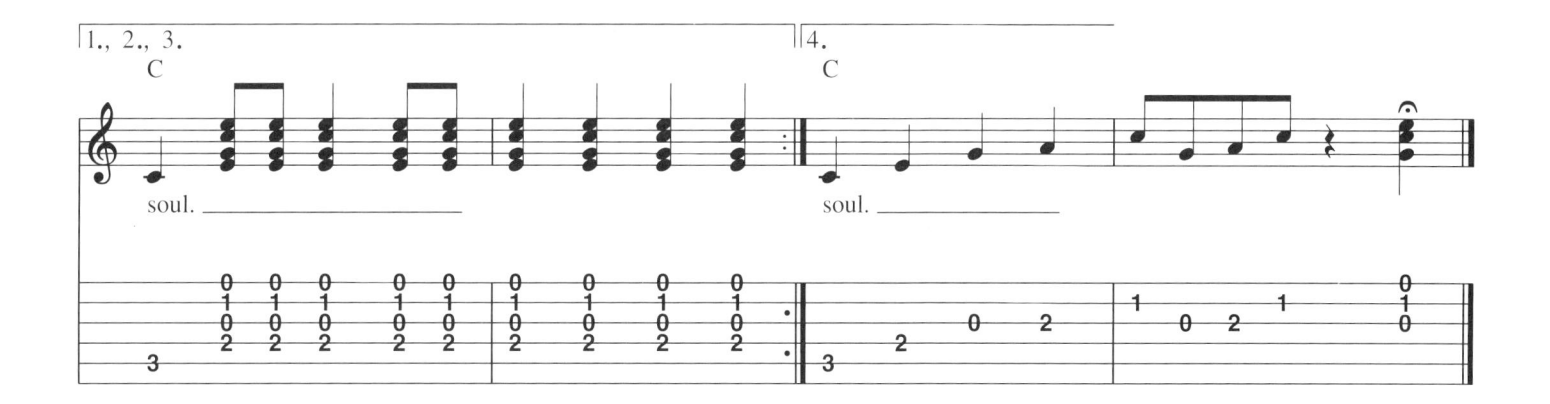

Additional Lyrics

2. Wearin' those dresses, your hair done up so right.
   Wearin' those dresses, your hair done up so right;
   You look so warm, but your heart is cold as ice.

3. I'm like a one-eyed cat, peepin' in a seafood store.
   I'm like a one-eyed cat, peepin' in a seafood store;
   I can look at you, tell you don't love me no more.

4. I believe you're doing me wrong and now I know.
   I believe you're doing me wrong and now I know;
   The more I work, the faster my money goes.

Susie-Q

Words and Music by Dale Hawkins, Stan Lewis and Eleanor Broadwater

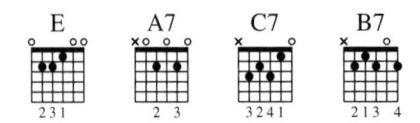

Chords: E, A7, C7, B7

Strum Pattern: 3
Pick Pattern: 3

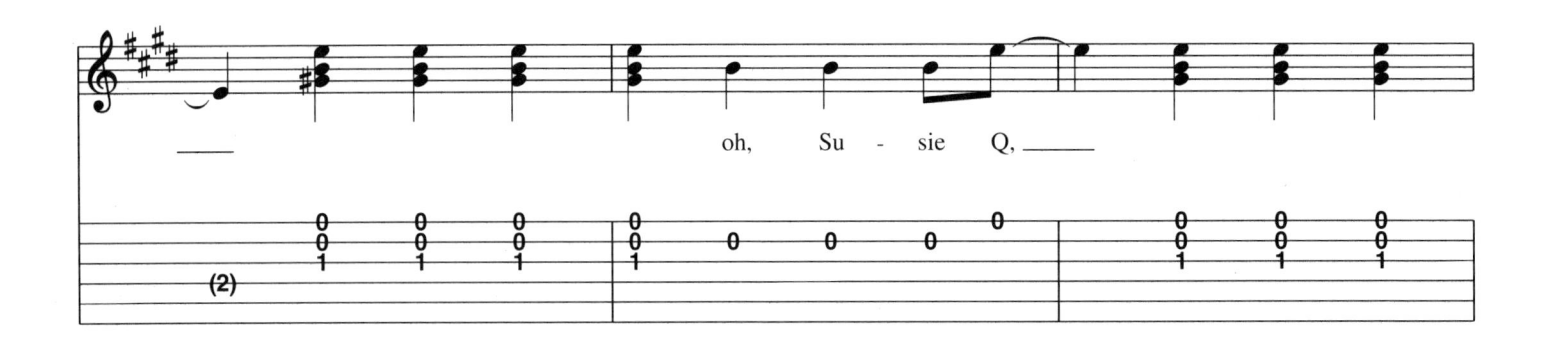

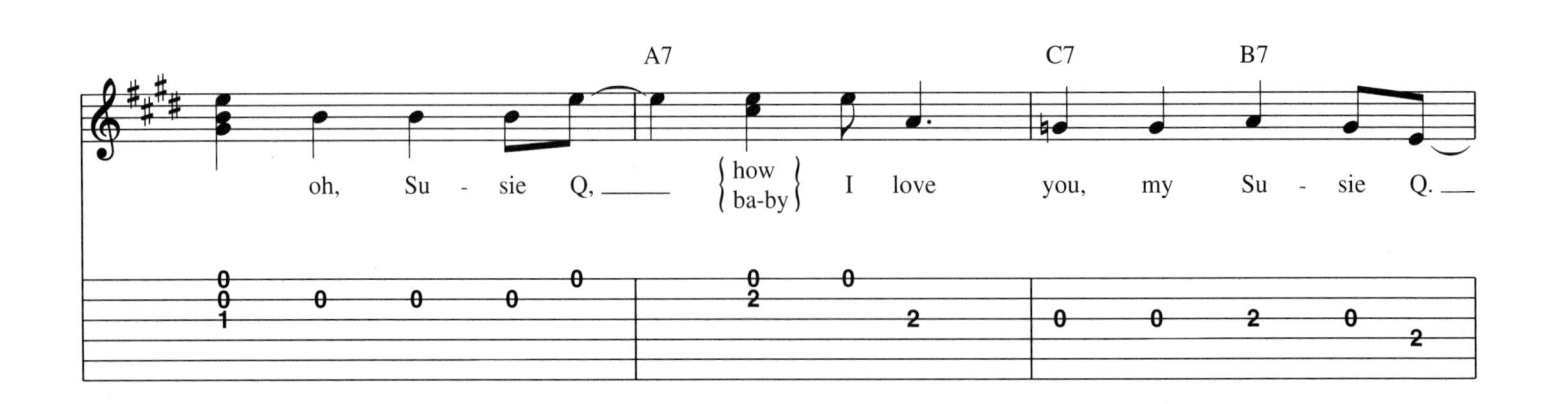

Intro
Moderate Rock

Chorus (play 4 times)

Oh, Su - sie Q, ___ oh, Su - sie Q, ___ oh, Su - sie Q, ___ {how baby} I love you, my Su - sie Q. ___

Copyright © 1957 (Renewed) by Arc Music Corporation (BMI)
International Copyright Secured   All Rights Reserved
Used by Permission

Additional Lyrics

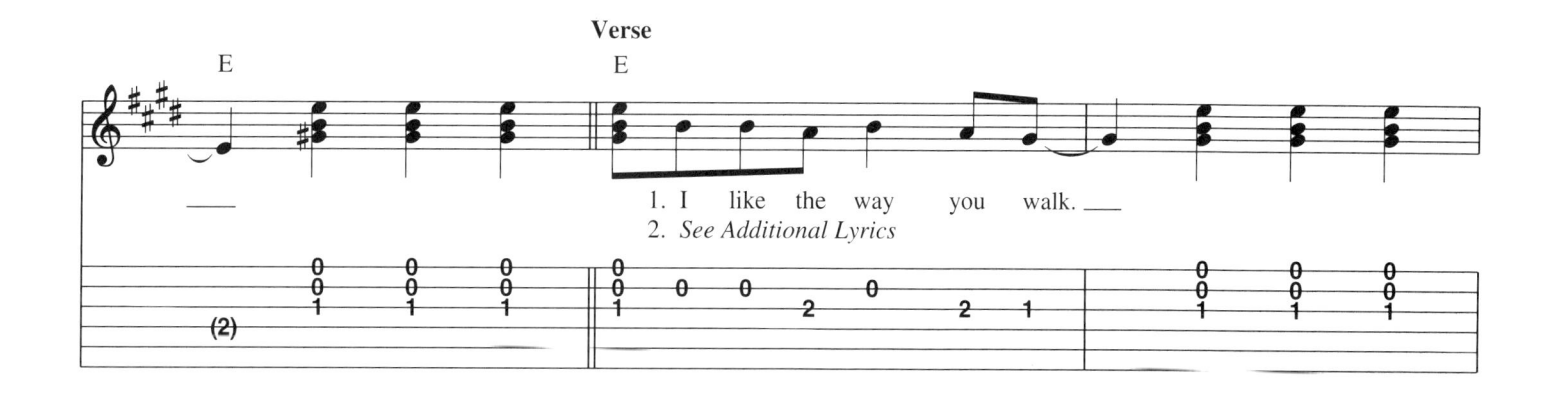

2. Well, say that you'll be true.
   Well, say that you'll be true.
   Well, say that you'll be true
   And never leave me blue,
   My Susie Q.

That'll Be the Day

Words and Music by Jerry Allison, Norman Petty and Buddy Holly

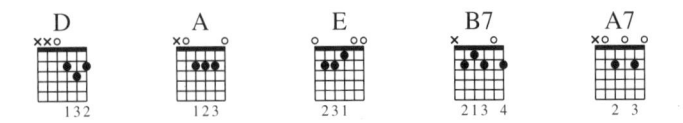

D A E B7 A7

Strum Pattern: 1
Pick Pattern: 2

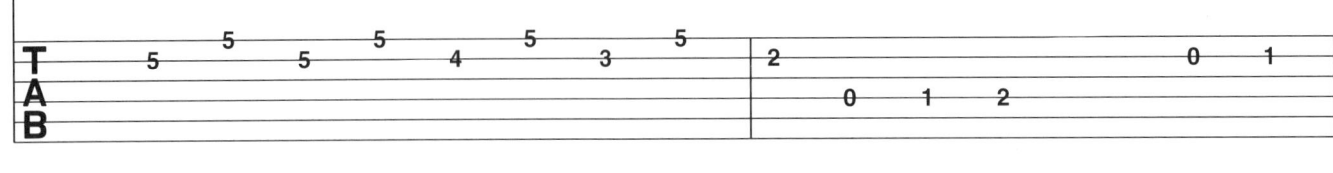

Intro
Moderately

Well,

Chorus

D   A
that-'ll be the day, when you say good-bye. Yes, that-'ll be the day, when

                                D
you make me cry. You say you're gon-na leave, you know it's a lie, ___ 'cause

© 1957 (Renewed) MPL COMMUNICATIONS, INC. and WREN MUSIC CO.
All Rights Reserved

To Coda

A that-'ll be the day ____ **E** when I die. ____ **A** 1. Well, you
2. *See Additional Lyrics*

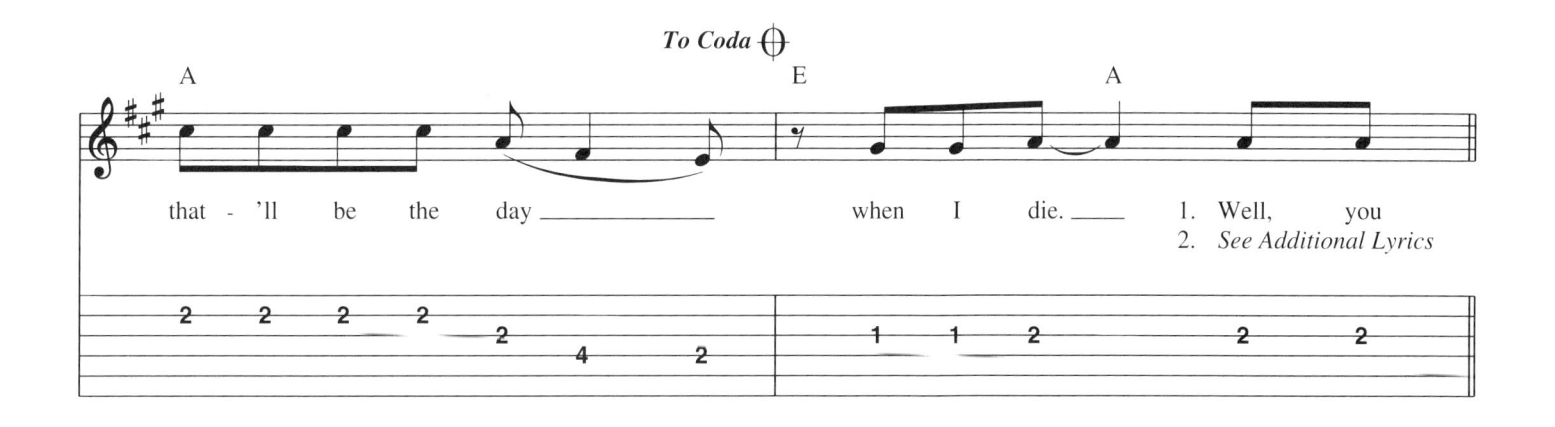

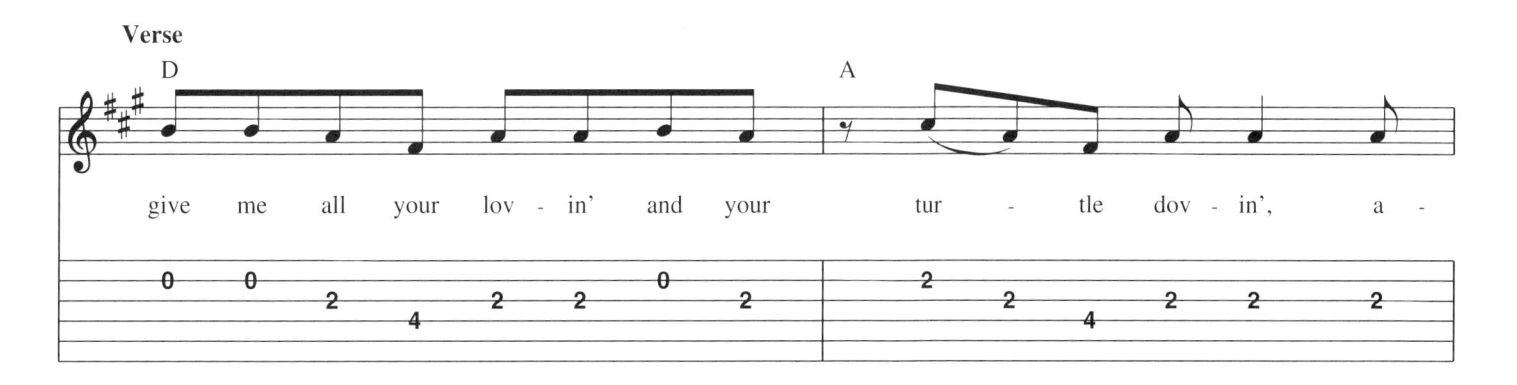

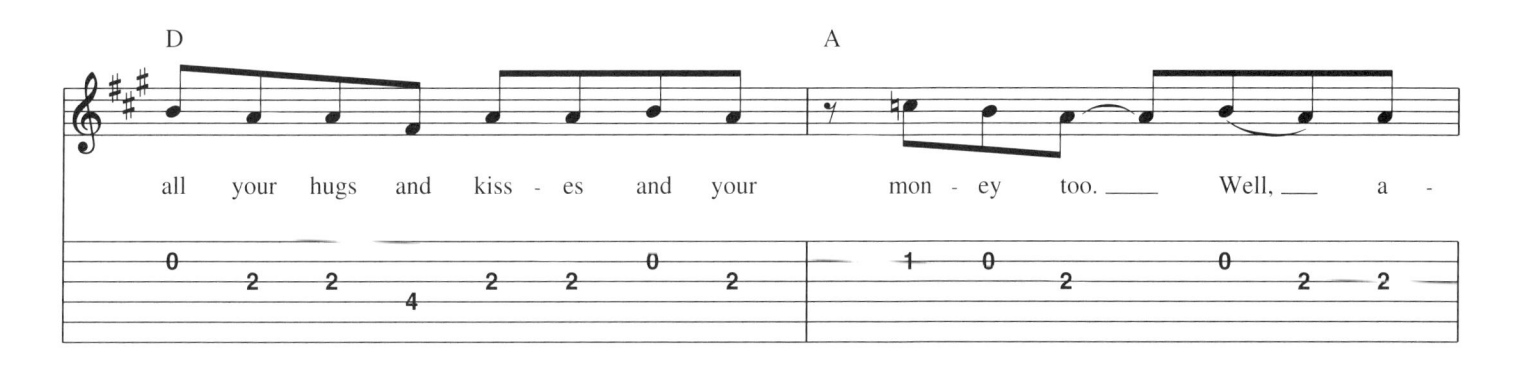

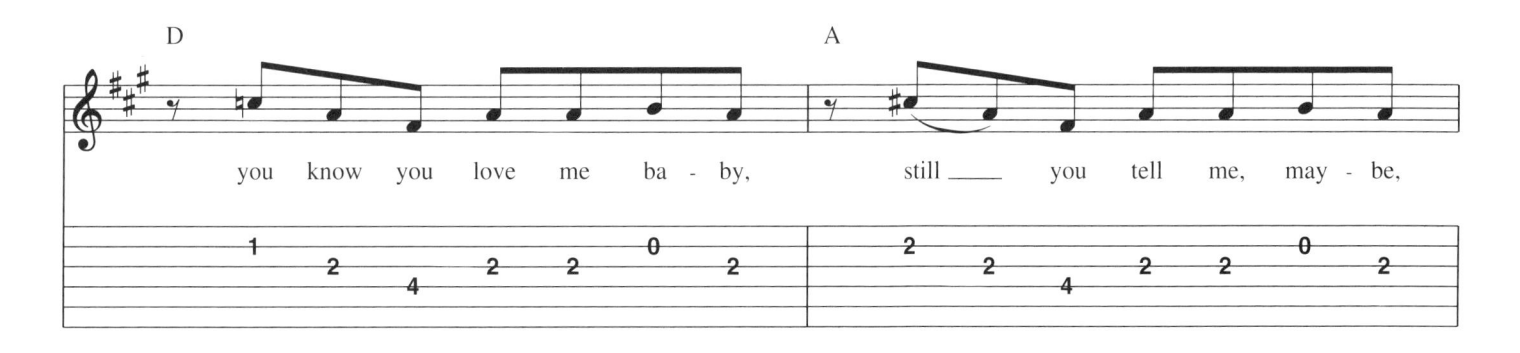

Verse

D give me all your lov-in' and your **A** tur-tle dov-in', a-

D all your hugs and kiss-es and your **A** mon-ey too. ____ Well, ____ a-

D you know you love me ba-by, **A** still ____ you tell me, may-be,

2nd time, D.S. al Coda

B7 that some day, well, **E** I'll be blue. ____ Well, ____

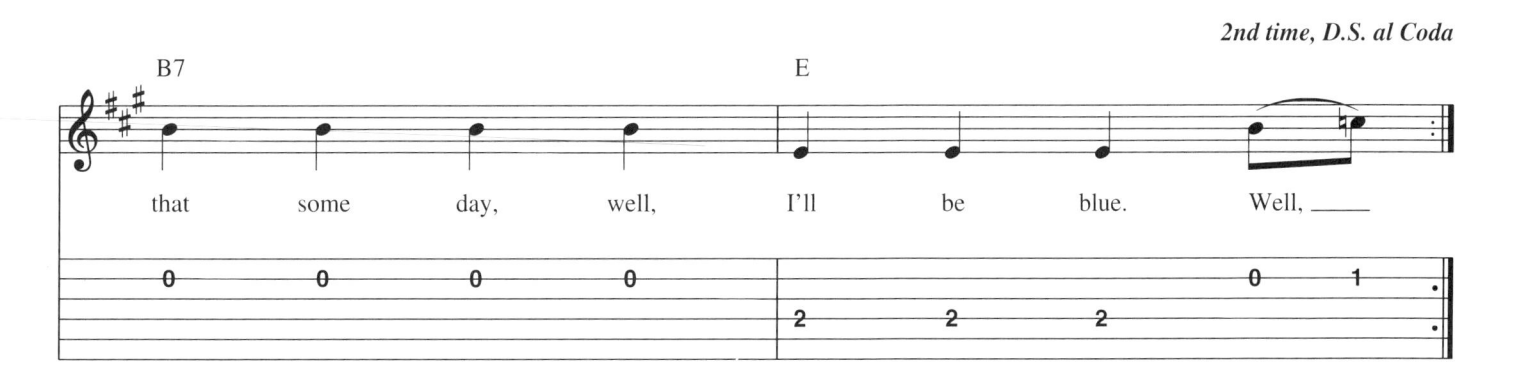

57

Additional Lyrics

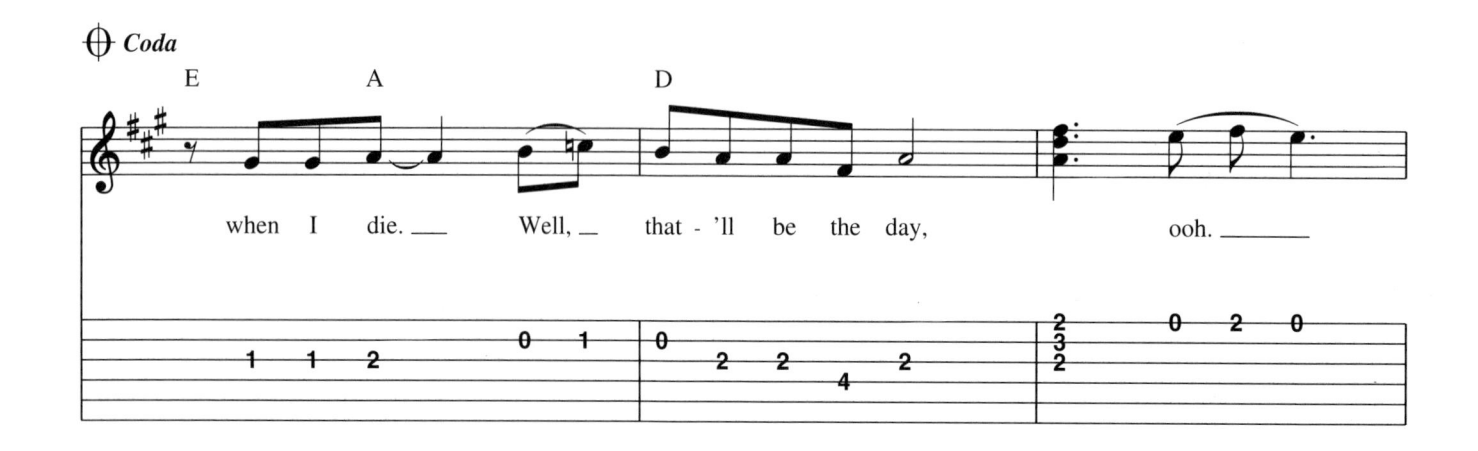

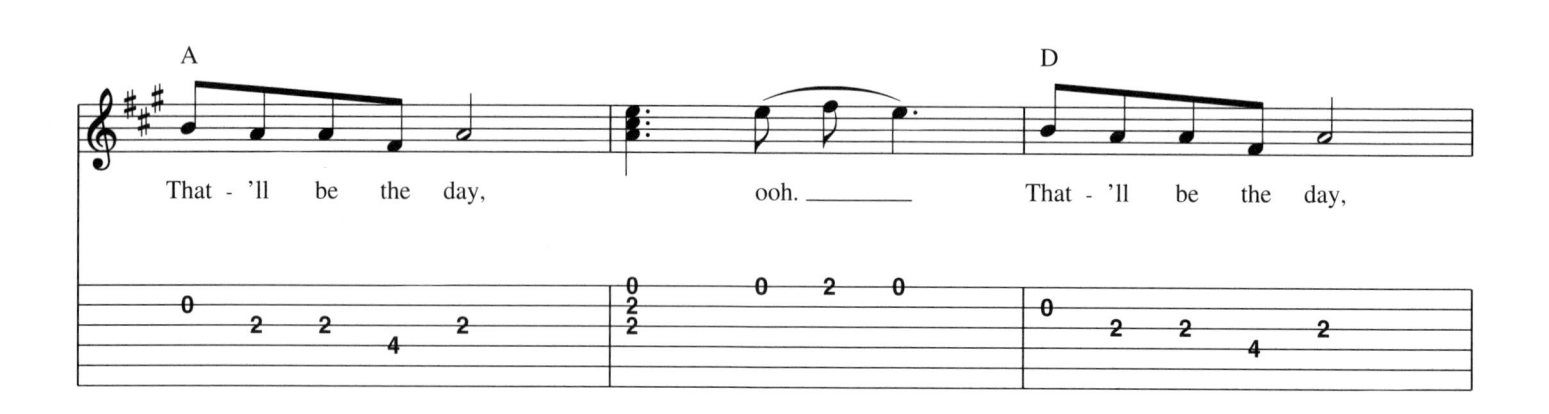

2. Well, when cupid shot his dart,
   He shot it at your heart,
   So if we ever part then I'll leave you.
   You sit and hold me and you
   Tell me boldly, that some day,
   Well, I'll be through.

Tutti Frutti

Words and Music by Richard Penniman and D. La Bostrie

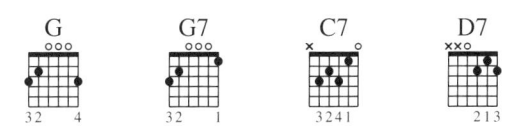

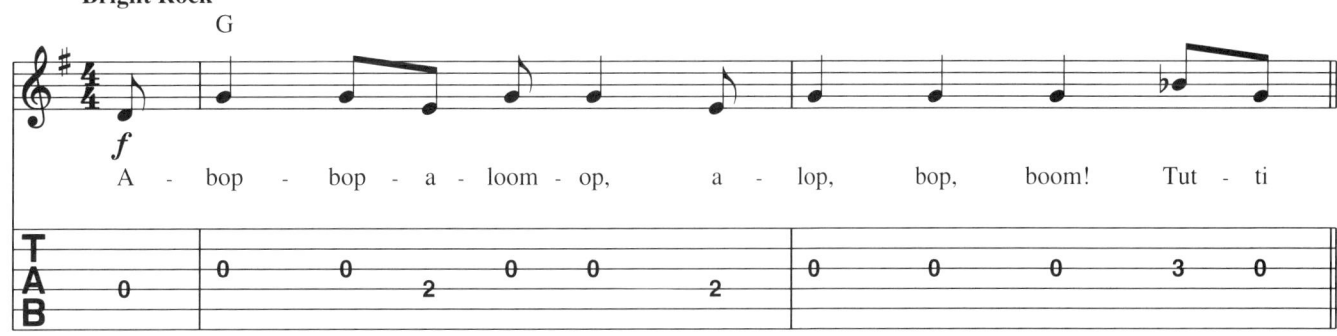

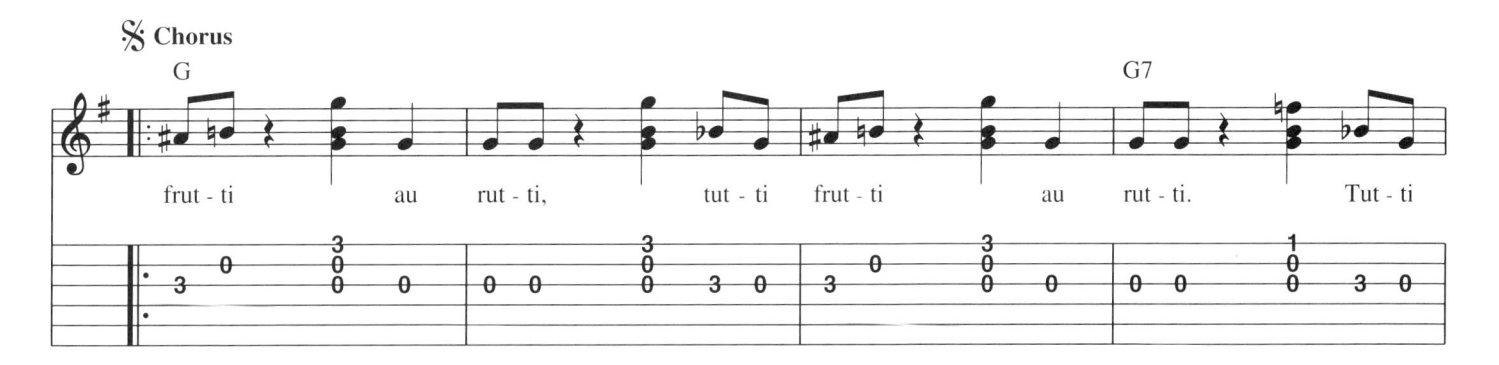

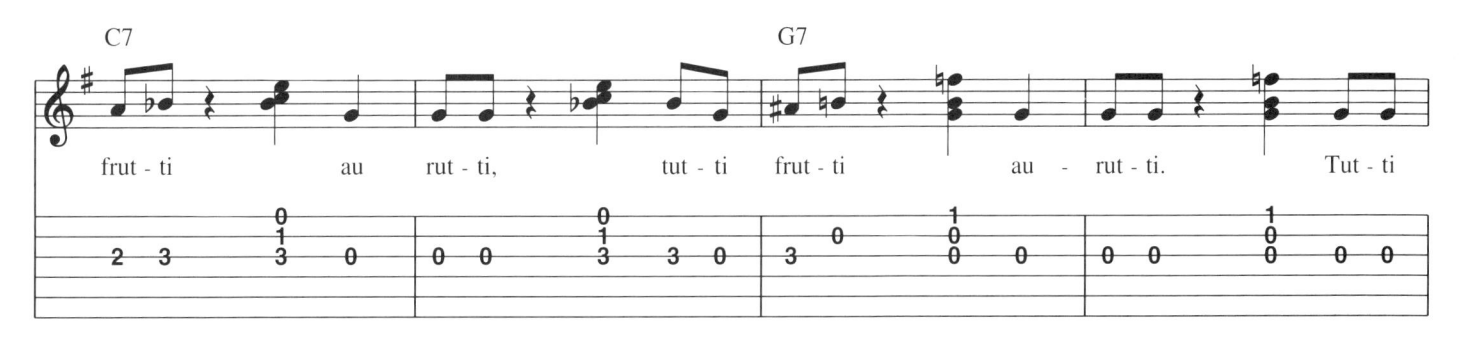

Strum Pattern: 1
Pick Pattern: 2

Intro
Bright Rock

A-bop - bop - a - loom - op, a - lop, bop, boom! Tut - ti

Chorus

frut - ti au rut - ti, tut - ti frut - ti au rut - ti. Tut - ti

frut - ti au rut - ti, tut - ti frut - ti au rut - ti. Tut - ti

To Coda

frut - ti au rut - ti, a - bop - bop, a - loom - op, a - lop, bop, boom! 1. I got a
2. *See Additional Lyrics*

© 1955 VENICE MUSIC CORP.
Copyright Renewed
All Rights Controlled and Administered by EMI BLACKWOOD MUSIC INC. under license from SONY/ATV SONGS LLC
All Rights Reserved International Copyright Secured Used by Permission

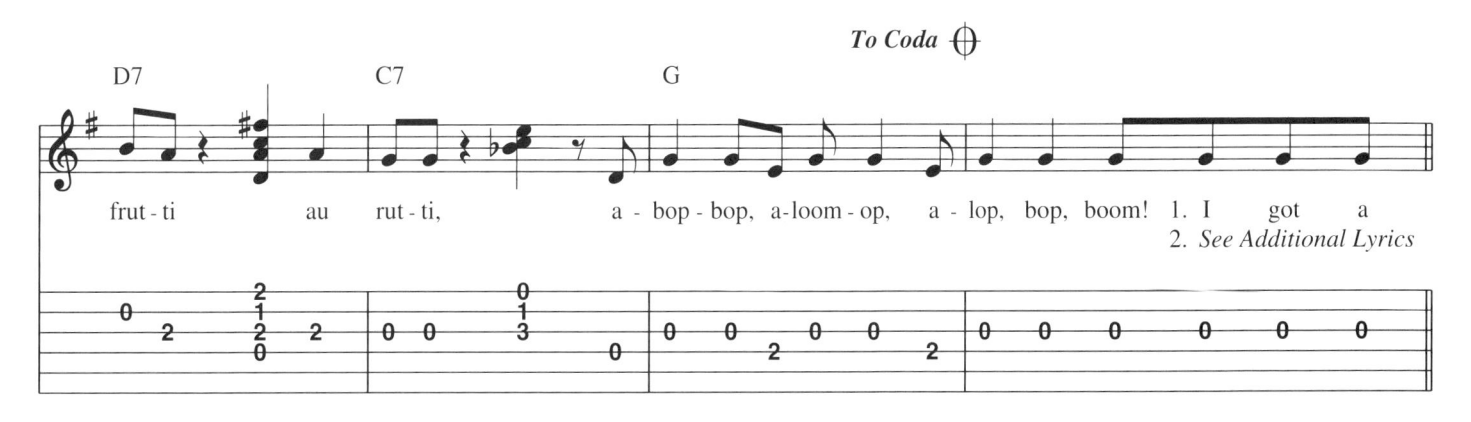

Verse

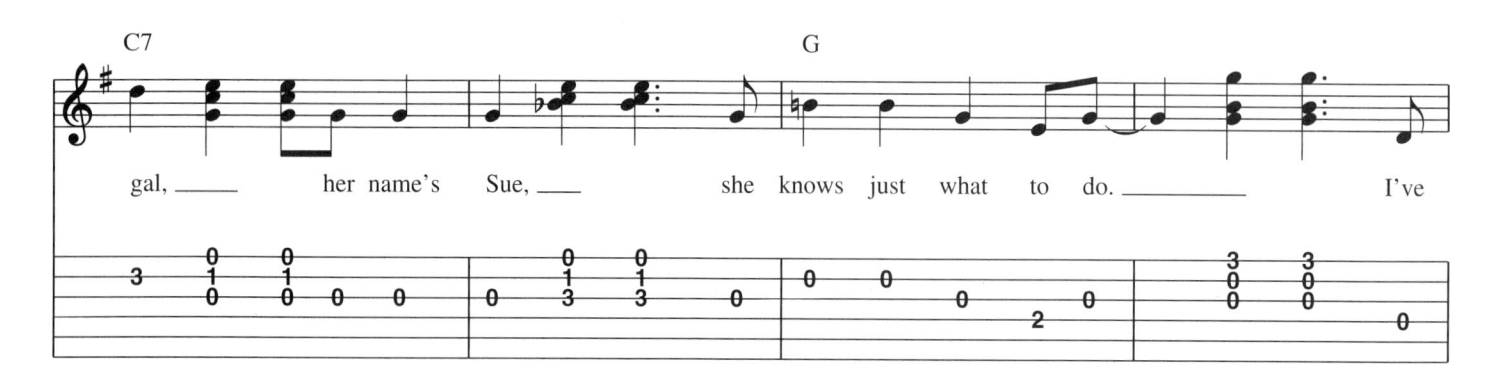

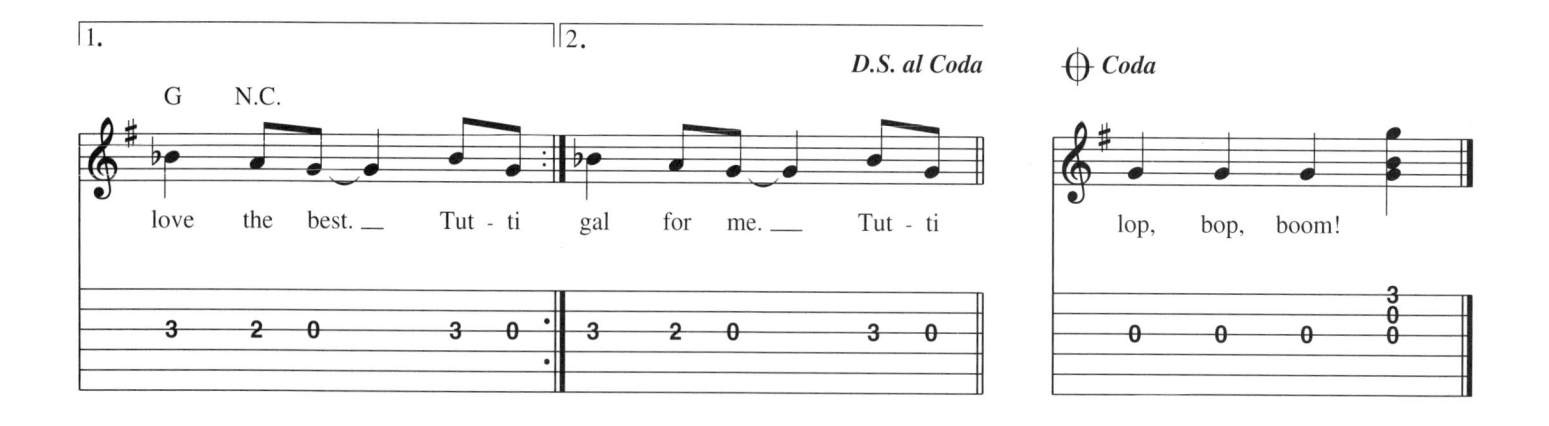

gal, her name's Sue, she knows just what to do, I got a gal, her name's Sue, she knows just what to do. I've been to the East, I've been to the West, But she's the gal I love the best. Tut-ti gal for me. Tut-ti lop, bop, boom!

D.S. al Coda — Coda

Additional Lyrics

2. I got a gal, her name's Daisy,
   She almost drives me crazy.
   I got a gal, her name's Daisy,
   She almost drives me crazy.
   She's a real gone cookie, yes sir ree,
   But pretty little Suzy's the gal for me.

Wake Up Little Susie

Words and Music by Boudleaux Bryant and Felice Bryant

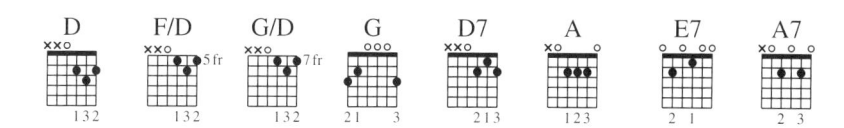

Strum Pattern: 1
Pick Pattern: 1

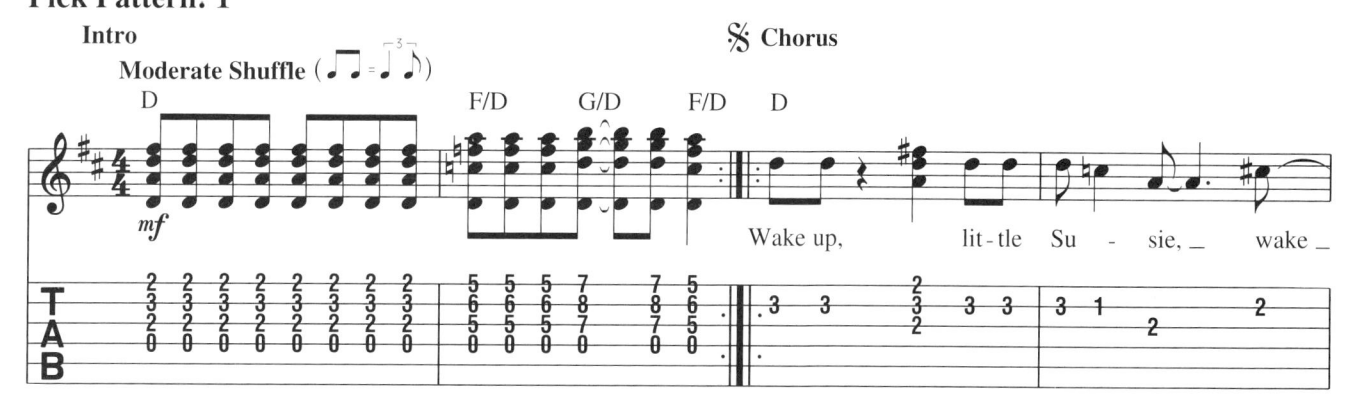

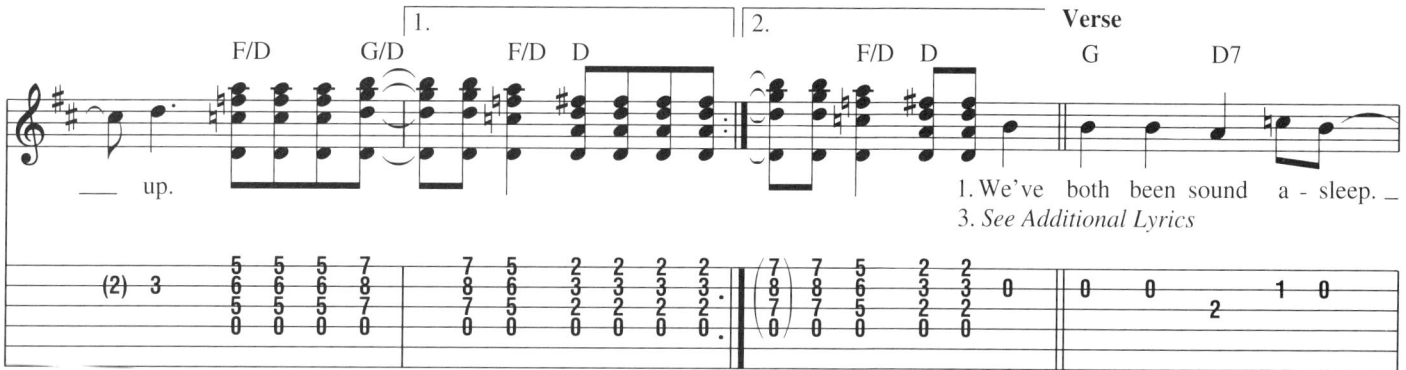

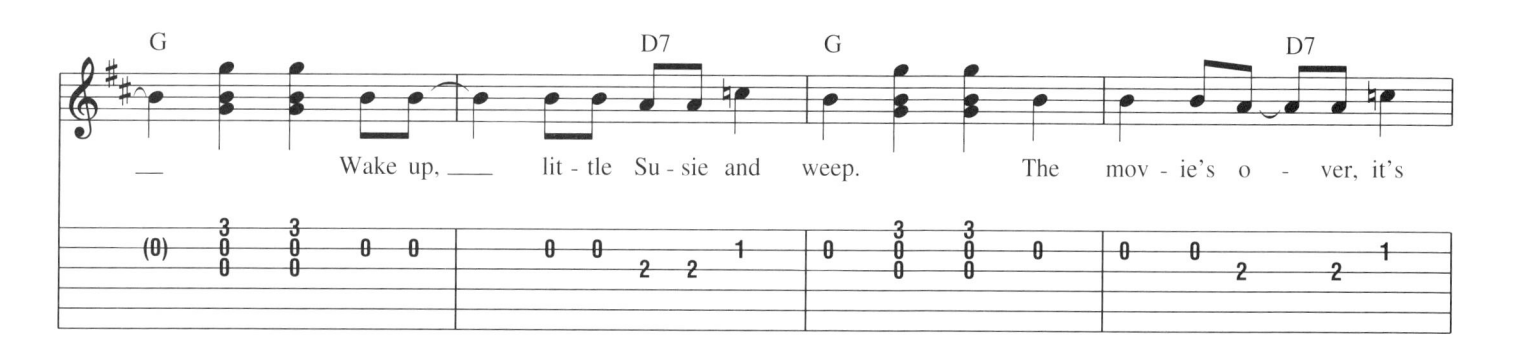

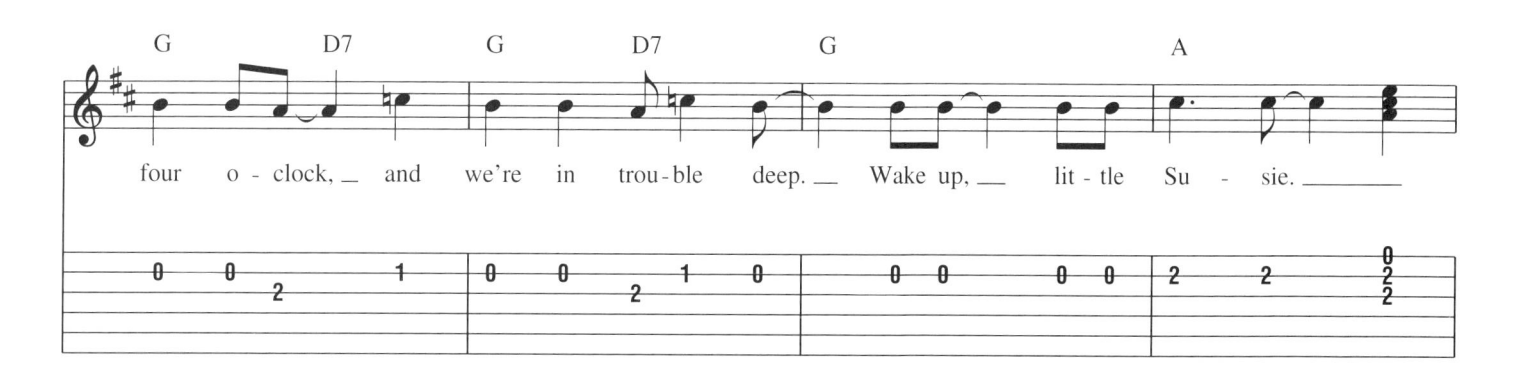

Verse
Bridge
To Coda
G A A E7 A E7 A E7 A A7 D A7 D D
Wake up, little Susie. 2., 4. Well, what-'re we gonna tell your mama?
What-'re we gonna tell your pa?
What-'re we gonna tell our friends when they say, "Ooh, la, la."
Wake up, little Susie. Wake up, little Susie.
Well, I told your mama that you'd be in by ten.

Additional Lyrics

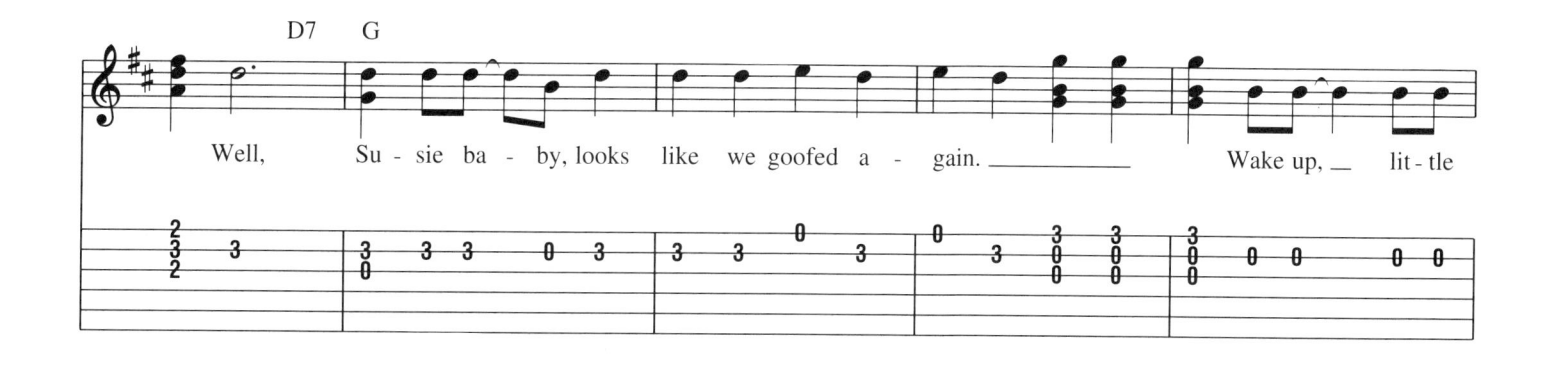

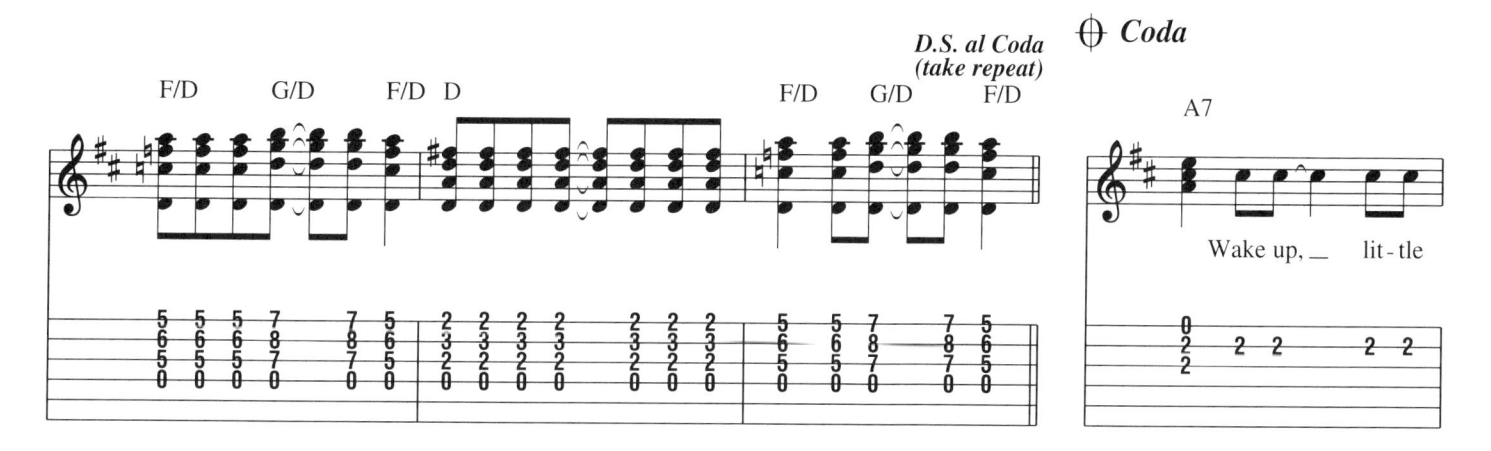

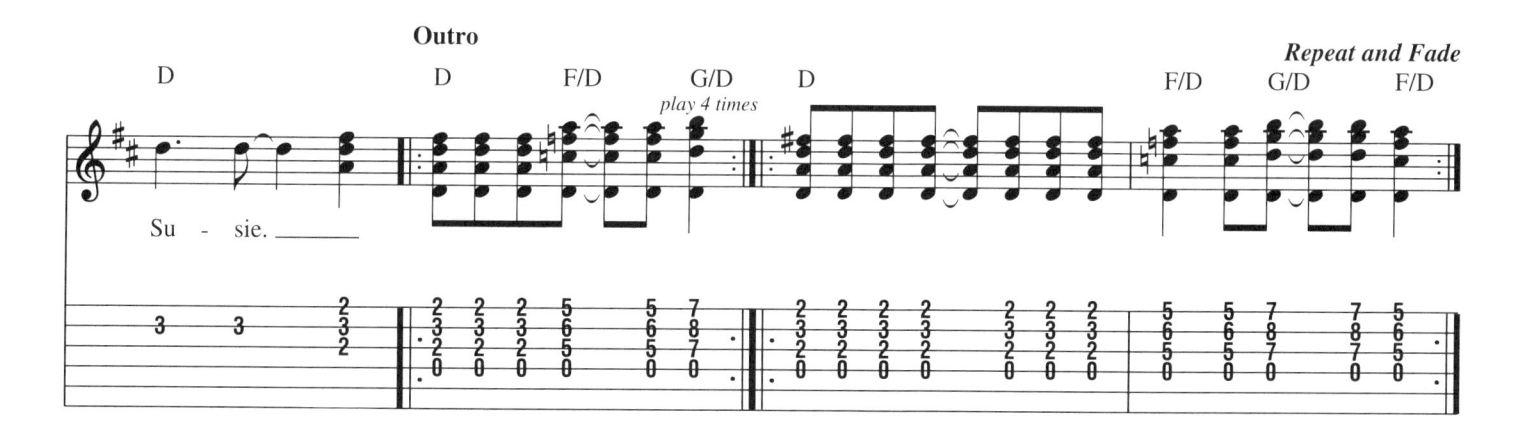

3. The movie wasn't so hot.
   It didn't have much of a plot.
   We fell asleep, our goose is cooked,
   Our reputation is shot.
   Wake up, little Susie.
   Wake up, little Susie.

STRUM AND PICK PATTERNS

This chart contains the suggested strum and pick patterns that are referred to by number at the beginning of each song in this book. The symbols ⊓ and ∨ in the strum patterns refer to down and up strokes, respectively. The letters in the pick patterns indicate which right-hand fingers plays which strings.

p = thumb
i = index finger
m = middle finger
a = ring finger

For example; Pick Pattern 2
is played: thumb - index - middle - ring

Strum Patterns / Pick Patterns

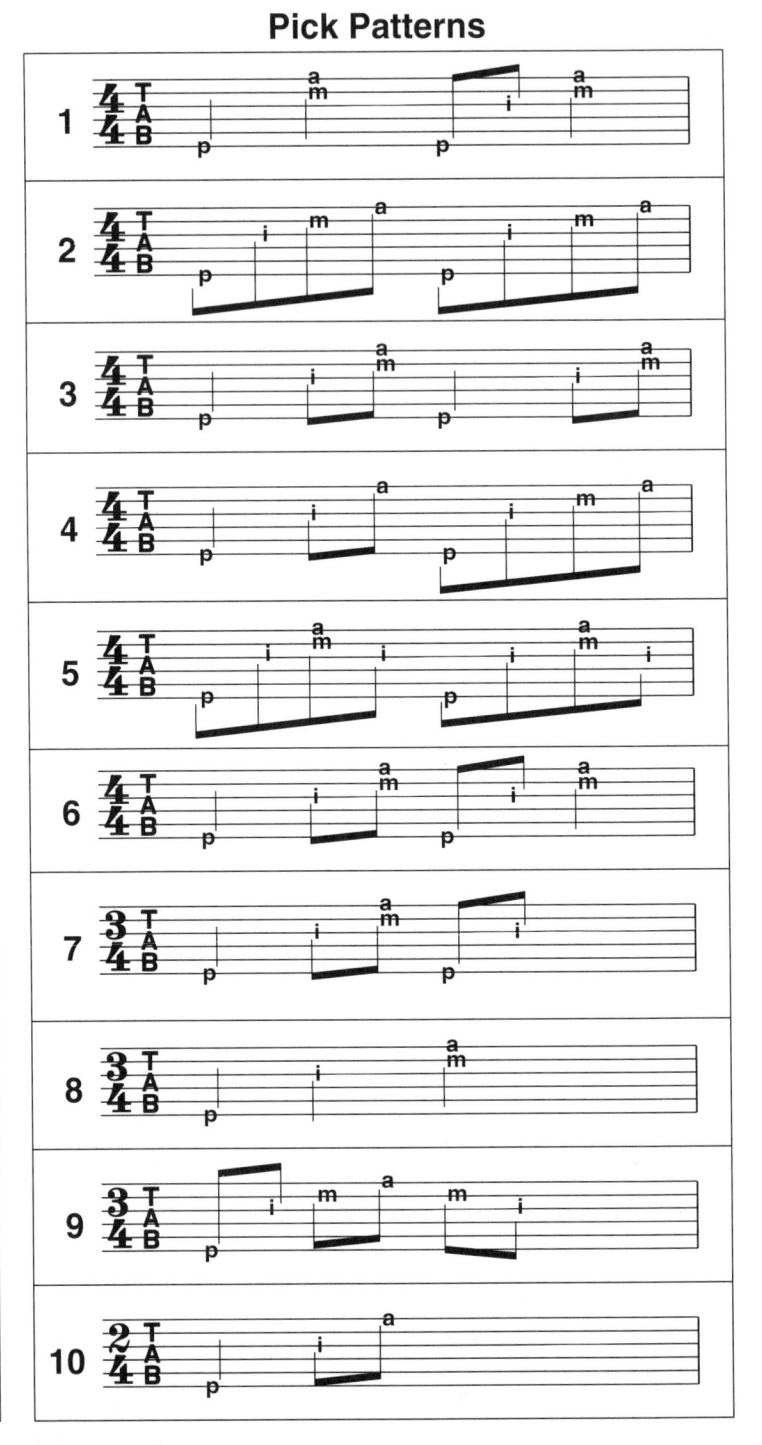

You can use the 3/4 Strum or Pick Patterns in songs written in compound meter (6/8, 9/8, 12/8, etc.). For example, you can accompany a song in 6/8 by playing the 3/4 pattern twice in each measure. The 4/4 Strum and Pick Patterns can be used for songs written in cut time (¢) by doubling the note time values in the patterns. Each pattern would therefore last two measures in cut time.

Hymns from the Classics

Words by John Waddington-Feather
Music by David Grundy

Published by Feather Books
PO Box 438
Shrewsbury SY3 0WN, UK
Tel/fax; 01743 872177

Website URL: http://www.waddysweb.freeuk.com
e-mail: john@waddysweb.freeuk.com

2005

The drawing on the front cover is of St. Chad's Church, Shrewsbury, reproduced by kind permission of the artist, Richard Moore.

ISBN: 1 84175 213 4

First published: 2005

All rights reserved

No part of this publication, which is copyright, may be reproduced or transmitted in any form or by any means, without prior permission of: Christian Copyright Licensing International Chantry House, 22 Upperton Rd, Eastbourne, E. Sussex BN21 1BF, U.K. Tele: 44 (0) 01323 417711 e-mail: info@ccli.co.uk

No. 7 in the Feather Books Music Series

HYMNS FROM THE CLASSICS

Following hard on their successful collection of new hymns, "Seasons and Occasions", (published by Feather Books in 2004) David Grundy and John Waddington-Feather have collaborated again to produce "Hymns from The Classics". In an inspired six months' work, from July 2004 to January 2005, they composed 50 new hymns all set to themes from classical music. They, like the first collection, cover most of the Church's calendar and other services in church.

An innovation in this collection are a couple of hymns which allow for choreography, now becoming popular as a form of liturgy. In the ancient Jewish church dancing was routine in worship. It was an expression of joy and praise. King David danced before the Lord (2 Samuel 6) and dancing was part of the liturgy of the Temple (Psalms 149 and 150). In our own age, dance is a completely natural part of Christian worship across Africa and elsewhere.

So well known are some of these tunes that we hope they will bring new life into church worship; that both congregational and choral worship will be fired by these new hymns and enjoy singing them to the Lord, as much as we enjoyed composing them for the Lord.

Most of the items in this collection are intended for congregational participation, but the following are recommended for choral use and as solos:-

No. 2	Almighty God	Tchaikowsky
No. 11	Give thanks unto the Lord	Mendelssohn
No. 12	Give thanks to God (alt. version)	Wagner
No. 22	Jesus, Lord	Mozart
No. 27	Lord God our Redeemer	Albinoni
No. 29	O, Christ the King	Berlioz

Solo Songs

No. 28	Lord Jesus, ever constant	Tchaikowsky
No. 30	O, God our Father	Handel
No. 33	O, happy day (Wedding Hymn)	Weber
No. 44	That Passiontide	Dvorak

D.G & J.W-F. (2005)

Hymns from the Classics
Index of First Lines and Sources

First Line	Source	Composer	No.
All good folk - *Christmas*	English Trad. "The Cuckoo"		1
Almighty God - *Praise Hymn*	Serenade for Strings (2nd Mt)	Tchaikowsky	2
As we draw near - *Evening*	Scottish Folksong		3
Be joyful - *Praise Hymn*	Piano Sonata Op. 90 (2nd Mt)	Beethoven	4
Blessed Apostle – *St. Paul*	"Pieds en l'air" (*Capriol Suite*)	Warlock, Peter	5
Bring us Lord – *Communion*	Nocturne (Midsummer Night's Dream)	Mendelssohn	6
Come, sing a song - *Praise*	Symphony No. 100 ("The Military")	Haydn	7
Dearest Saviour – *Prayer*	Symphony No. 9 ("The Great") 2nd Mt.	Schubert	8
Deep the rolling river – *Praise*	Cello Concerto (1st Mt.)	Dvorak	9
Fearless did the Apostle – *St. Stephen*	Melody "Tom Bowling"	Dibdin, Charles	10
Give thanks - *Praise*	Cantata "Hymn of Praise"	Mendelssohn	11
Give thanks to God – *Praise*	Pilgrims' Chorus (*Tannhäuser*)	Wagner	12
God our Creator – *Creation*	Symphony No. 5 (2nd Mt.)	Tchaikowsky	13
Golden the Harvest – *Harvest*	Symphony No. 6 ("Pastoral") 5th Mt.	Beethoven	14
Hail, Christ – *Easter*	Pavane (*Capriol Suite*)	Warlock, Peter	15
Happy those people – *General*	*Entr'acte* from "Rosamunde"	Schubert	16
Holy Spirit – *Communion*	Symphony No. 9 (Finale)	Beethoven	17
How beautiful this England – *National*	Symphonic Poem *Vltava*	Smetana	18
Idyllic summer day – *Thanksgiving*	Symphonic Poem *Bohemia's Meadows*	Smetana	19
In all of our learning – *Wisdom*	*Academic Festival* Overture	Brahms	20
Jesus, good Lord – *Penitence*	"Earl of Salisbury's Pavane"	Byrd, William	21
Jesus, Lord – *Pentecost*	"March of the Priests" (*Magic Flute*)	Mozart	22
Lead us, daily – *Prayer*	Romanza from Horn Concerto K.447	Mozart	23
Let us all rejoice – *Praise*	*Academic Festival* Overture	Brahms	24
Let us dance - *Dance*	"Gavotte" from *Holberg Suite*	Grieg	25
Lord God – *General*	Sonata *Pathétique* (2nd Mt.)	Beethoven	26
Lord God, our Redeemer – *Lent*	*Adagio*	Albinoni	27
Lord Jesus, ever constant – *General*	Symphony No. 6 (*Pathétique*)	Tchaikowsky	28
O Christ the King – *Praise*	Carnival Romain Overture	Berlioz	29
O God our Father - *General*	Aylesford Pieces	Handel	30
O Jesus, my Saviour - *Healing*	Symphony No. 1 (Finale)	Brahms	31
O rejoice – *Praise*	Quintet for Piano and Wind, K. 452	Mozart	32
O, happy day – *Wedding*	Oberon Overture	Weber	33
One God, One Christ – *Trinity*	Symphony No. 3 (*Scottish*), Finale	Mendelssohn	34
Our Saviour is beside us – *General*	"The Lime Tree" (*Winter Journey*)	Schubert	35
Peace comes into the soul – *Prayer*	Piano Concerto No. 5 (2nd Mt.)	Beethoven	36
Praise our God – **Praise**	Duet from *The Pearl Fishers*	Bizet	37
Praise we our Lord – *Praise*	Piano Sonata D.959 (1st Mt.)	Schubert	38
Save us, O Christ - *Mental Health*	Symphony No. 2 (2nd Mt.)	Beethoven	39
Shepherdman – **Bereavement**	Symphony No. 9 (*New World*) (2nd Mt)	Dvorak	40
Sing aloud – **Dance**	Scottish Folksong "Kelvingrove"		41
Sing high, sing low – *Praise*	Symphony No. 3 (*Eroica*) (Finale)	Beethoven	42
Sing, O sing – *Dance*	*Harmonious Blacksmith* Variations	Handel	43
That Passiontide – *Easter*	Symphony No. 5 (2nd Mt.)	Dvorak	44
The morning has broken – *Morning*	Symphony No. 88 (2nd Mt.)	Haydn	45
There in the morning – *General*	*Zemir et Azore*	Grétry	46
This pleasant land – *National*	Violin Concerto No. 2 (2nd Mt.)	Bruch M.	47
Welcome in the harvest – *Harvest*	St. Anthony Chorale	Haydn	48
When God came down – *Advent*	Symphony No. 4 (*Italian*) (2nd Mt)	Mendelssohn	49
When St. Peter – *Apostles*	Symphony No. 7 (2nd Mt.)	Dvorak	50

All good folk
(English Folksong*) a Song for Christmas

Flowing, not too slow
May be sung in four-part harmony

Words: John Waddington-Feather
Music: arr. David Grundy

1. All good folk come a-long and I'll sing you a song of a Sav-iour who came long a-go, long a-go. He was born next an inn, which would not take him in, and his moth-er did lay him so low in a mang-er with catt-le so low.

2. He was Christ, God's own Son, the div-ine chos-one sent to earth to re-deem all be-low; all be-low; but was nailed on a cross, while the sold-iers did toss for his garm-ents and mocked him be-low and the hol-y ones scorned him be-low.

3. Jesus rose from the dead
resurrected, the head
of the Church that he founded below.
He confounded them all,
and holds Satan in thrall,
sent to hell where the evil ones go..........
sent to hell in the depths far below.

4. Now Christ reigns here for aye
from his throne up on high,
as the Lord of creation below;
where he lives with us still,
and his Spirit does fill
those who follow and love him below..........
those who love and adore him below.

*English Folksong "The Cuckoo and the Nightingale"

Copyright Words: John Waddngton-Feather 2004
Music: David Grundy 2004

Praise Chorus
Elegy, from Serenade for Strings
TCHAIKOWSKY 1840-93   With optional instrumental part

Words: John Waddington-Feather
Music: David Grundy

Andante

Organ Intro.

Al-might-y God is great, Sur-passing all our prais - es; En-throned in high-est

Optional instrumental part

heav'n, There up-on high, be-yond all earth - ly thought

Through Jes - us Christ, his Son, Who came from heav'n to save us, And

This piece may be performed by a soloist, with either organ accompaniment, or with unaccompanied, humming chorus. The instrumental part may be played by a violin or flute

Copyright words: John Waddington-Feather 2004
music: David Grundy 2004

No. 11 Praise Chorus, Contd (2)

bring us a-gain to God; And re-store us once more in Him; To raise us up from mire-ful sin And lead us cleansed back home.

Repeat ad lib.

EVENING HYMN
Scottish Folksong

3

Flowing

May be sung in four-part harmony

Words: John Waddington-Feather
Music: arr. David Grundy

As we draw near the night, Lord God be with us;
As even-ing shad-ows fall, Lord God, be with us
Grant us peace that we may sleep free from fear, that we may rise
act-ive, re-stored in you, Lord God be with us.

2. When dark clouds mask the sky,
Lord Christ be with us;
when glowing sunset fades,
Lord Christ be with us.
Bring us rest that we may sleep
free from harm, secure in Him.
As we retire this night
Saviour, be with us.

Feather Books
www.waddysweb.freeuk.com
Copyright Words: John Waddington-Feather 2004
Music: David Grundy 2004

A Hymn of Praise
Be Joyful
Piano Sonata Op. 90 (2nd Mt.) BEETHOVEN 1770-1827

Four-part harmony optional

Words: John Waddington-Feather
Music: arr. David Grundy

1. Be joy-ful and mer-ry and thank God for all his grace. O give thanks for his good-ness, man-i-fest in ev'-ry place. Praise God! give thanks! give thanks! Praise God! And wor-ship him in full-ness, peop-le all of ev'-ry race.

2. Sound trump-ets and ins-tru-ments in full praise to our King. And you viol-ins and sweet-est harps make musi-ic with your strings. Praise God! give thanks! give thanks! Praise God. Bow down be-fore his glor-y and your high-est trib-utes bring

3. You ten-ors and bass-es give your best in full acc-ord. And sop-ran-os and alt-os sing tri-umph-ant to the Lord. Praise God! give thanks! give thanks! Praise God! Great harm-on-ies of mus-ic rend your praise in ev'-ry chord!

Copyright Words: John Waddington-Feather 2005
Music: David Grundy 2005

The Conversion of St. Paul
"Pieds en l'air" from Capriol Suite, by Peter Warlock 1894-1930

Flowing
May be sung in four-part harmony

Words: John Waddington-Feather
Music: arr. David Grundy

slur for v. 3

Bless-ed Ap-ost-le, tire-less preacher of God's hol-y Word, Trav-ell-ing far and wide, the miss-ion-'ry of the Lord; Suff-'ring ship-wreck, scourging and pris-on, then fin-al-ly death, In-spir-ed ev-er, al-ways by the Spir-it's breath. Suff-'ring ship-wreck, scourging and pris-on, then final-ly death, In-spir-ed ev-er, al-ways by the Spir-it's breath.

2. On this his day, give thanks for life fulfilled in Saint Paul.
Labouring in the field to bring our Lord to all;
He himself, converted on the Damascus road,
Good Ananias freed him him from the pricking goad. *(Repeat the last two lines).*

3. Sightless, Saul's eyes were opened to the living Christ,
Who for his sins had paid the final sacrifice,
Rose from the dead, revealing himself to the hate-filled Saul,
Cleansed him from hatred, changing to a loving Paul. *(Repeat the last two lines).*

Copyright Words: John Waddington-Feather 2004
Music: David Grundy 2004

Gradual Communion Hymn
"Bring us, Lord"
Nocturne - "Midsummer Night's Dream" Music MENDELSSOHN

6

Andante con moto
Four-part harmony optional

Words: John Waddington-Feather
Music: arr. David Grundy

Bring us, Lord, in-to your Pres-ence Through bread and wine; Fill us with your Spir-it, Great Mast-er div-ine; Bring us, Lord, in-to your Pres-ence through pow-er of prayer, That knelt at Your Tab-le we meet with you there, And so in Com-mun-ion, Your Pres-ence we'll share.

Copyright words: John Waddington-Feather 2004
music: David Grundy 2004

Come, Sing a Song!
Symphony 100 "The Military" - HAYDN 1732-1809

To be sung in march-like tempo, in unison

Words: John Waddington-Feather
Music: arr. David Grundy

Come, sing a song for Jesus, Christians! Sing a merry song for Jesus, Sing aloud your joy, make a merry noise with all your heart! Sing, sing aloud you choirs with songs of gladness and raise your joyful anthems here with sweet notes of praise. So each one sing, each Christian, Sing a happy song for Jesus, Tell the whole wide world our Saviour Jesus Christ is Lord!

Copyright words: John Waddington-Feather 2004
music: David Grundy 2004

Dearest Saviour
8   Symphony No. 9 ("The Great") (2nd Mt) SCHUBERT 1797-1828

Andante con moto
Four-part harmony optional

Words: John Waddington-Feather
Music: Arr. David Grundy

Dear-est Saviour, keep your pres-ence near us,
Leave us not a-lone, but be with us al-way;
Re-vive our flag-ging spir-its and our faith, we pray.

2. Dear Lord Jesus, ever our life's Shepherd,
When Temptation comes, be ever our true Guide,
Give us strength to stay, Lord,
Firmly at your side

3. Friend and Master, Comforter in sickness,
Healer of our sins and Saviour of each soul,
Guide through death's dark valley
With you, fully whole.

Copyright words: John Waddington-Feather 2004
music: David Grundy 2004

Deep the Rolling River
9   Cello Concerto (1st Mt.) - DVORAK 1841-1904

Andante con moto
May be sung in unison, or as a solo song

Words: John Waddington-Feather
Music: arr. David Grundy

1. Deep the rolling river
   and high the endless sky,
   so bountiful the Giver,
   Creator God on high;
   so bountiful the Giver,
   Creator God in heaven.

2. Wild the foaming ocean
   and blistering desert sand;
   yet all give you devotion
   and work to your command;
   yet all give you devotion
   and all work to your planning.

3. We, e'en we, his creatures,
   surrounded by his love,
   each single person features
   in his great scheme above;
   each single person features
   in his great scheme almighty.

4. Let us sound our praises,
   and thanks for holding us dear;
   our God the one who raises
   our hope and trusting here;
   our God the one who raises
   our hope and trust while living.

Feather Books
www.waddysweb.freeuk.com
Copyright Words: John Waddington-Feather 2004
Music: David Grundy 2004

St. Stephen's Day Gradual
Melody "Tom Bowling" by Charles Dibdin (1745-1814)

Moderate tempo
May be sung in four-part harmony

Words: John Waddington-Feather
Music: arr. David Grundy

Fear-less did the good Saint Steph-en Preach the Word to his foes; A-gain, a-gain he spoke of Jes-us, How he rose from death to de-liv-er us, They dis-missed his preach-ing, stoned him, but he, for-giv-ing, heav'n-wards rose.

www.waddysweb.freeuk.com
Copyright words: John Waddington-Feather 2004
music: David Grundy 2004

Give Thanks
From "Hymn of Praise" - Mendelssohn 1809-47
An Anthem

Words: John Waddington-Feather
Music: arr. David Grundy

Andante

Solo Voice

Give thanks un-to the Lord, O give thanks un-to his name, And praise Him for His bless-ings a-gain and a-gain; A-dore His glor-ious Name, it re-mains for ev-er sure, He al-ways, for ev-er

Copyright Words: John Waddngton-Feather 2005
Music: David Grundy 2005

No. 11 Hymn of Praise - Contd. (2)

keeps us se-cure And holds us ev-er close, give thanks to His Name And holds us ev-er close, give thanks to His Name

Chorus optional

Descant
We thank our Sav-iour Christ, sent from heav'n a-bove,

Men's Voices
We thank our Sav-iour Christ, Sent to earth from heav'n a-bove, Give

No. 11 Hymn of Praise Contd. (3)

Give thanks that God's Son hung on the tree,
thanks that God's dear Son hung high on the tree, He
He died upon the Cross, an un-end-ing sign of love, He
died up-on the Cross, an un-end-ing sign of love, He burst forth the
burst from death once for all. Give thanks, give
bonds of death once for all. Give thanks un-to the Lord, give

No. 11 Hymn of Praise Contd. (4)

thanks to His Name. Give thanks un-to the Lord, give

thanks to His Name

Give Thanks to God

Pilgrims' Chorus ("Tannhauser") by WAGNER

Words: John Waddington-Feather
Music: arr. David Grundy

Give thanks to God; let us all praise Him for ev-er, Your Name, O God, is a-bove all Cre-a-tion; Let all bless you, our God, Let all hon-our your Name; Your great-ness is un-bound-ed; be-yond mort-al praise. All your saints cry a-loud; They ex-tol your great acts. And they tell of your King-dom and your might-y power, Your Name al-ways for aye we

Repeat in Unison, or use following, alternative version.

praise, for ev-er and ev-er your name we praise.
(Give,...(alt.version)

Copyright words: John Waddington-Feather 2004
music: David Grundy 2004

No. 12 Give thanks - contd (2)

Give thanks to Christ, who was sent down by our Father, To save mankind here on the Cross as our Redeemer; Jesus died for our sins, To restore us to life. Man-

Four-part chorus

No. 12 Give thanks- Contd.(3)

kind, lift up your voic -es and pour forth your praise Hal - le - lu -

ja! Hal - le - lu - jah Then let us give our

thanks and praise un - to you, O Lord.

13 Kyrie Eleison - God our Creator (Praise Hymn)
From the 2nd Mt. of Symphony No. 5 - TCHAIKOWSKY 1840-93

Optional four-part Harmony
Slos, but 2 beats to the bar

Words: John Waddington-Feather
Music: arr. David Grundy

Lyrics (verse 1 / verse 2):

God our Cre - a - tor, God our Red - eem - er, Our on - ly Cre - a - tor, Red - eem - er, Com - fort and Guide at life's end - ing, God our Def - end - er, God our Sal - vat - ion, Streng - then our faith in your life e - ter - nal. Our ebb - ing spir - it craves your com - pass - ion, be with us caught in the snares of Death.

Bless - ed Lord Jes - us, Broth - er and Sav - iour, Hold us close Lord Jes - us, and Sav - iour, when our life light is fad - ing. Bless - ed Lord Jes - us, Lord Jes - us ev - er be near us, Lead us to heav'n when Death's shad - ow lies o'er us. Gent - le Lord Jes - us, our lov - ing Mast - er, Bring us each one to our home with you.

Copyright words: John Waddington-Feather 2004
music: DAvid Grundy 2004

Harvest Thanksgiving Hymn
14   Symphony No. 6 ("Pastoral") BEETHOVEN 1770-1827

Flowing, may be sung in unison
2 beats to the bar

Words: John Waddington-Feather
Music: arr. David Grundy

Optional instrumental part

vv. 1, 3, 5 Unison

1. Golden the harvest and bright the fields of corn, Right heavy the grain gathered to the silos borne.
3. Weary the farmer and tired the farmer's man, Unloading the corn, ripe into the brimming barn,
5. Lord of the harvest, who gives with bounteous hand, We thank you for many the blessings on our land.

Optional instrumental part.

Harmony

2. Backwards and forwards the growling tractors go, Alongside the combines that reap each yielding row.
4. Morning till nightfall, they toil to bring it home, Our food from the rich soil, our bread from the loam.
6. Thank you, our Father, who strives to keep us whole, With bread for the body and food for the soul.

D.C.

Copyright Words: John Waddngton-Feather 2004
Music: David Grundy 2004

Easter Morning Hymn
Hail, Christ This Glorious Morn
"Capriol Suite" - Peter Warlock 1894-1930

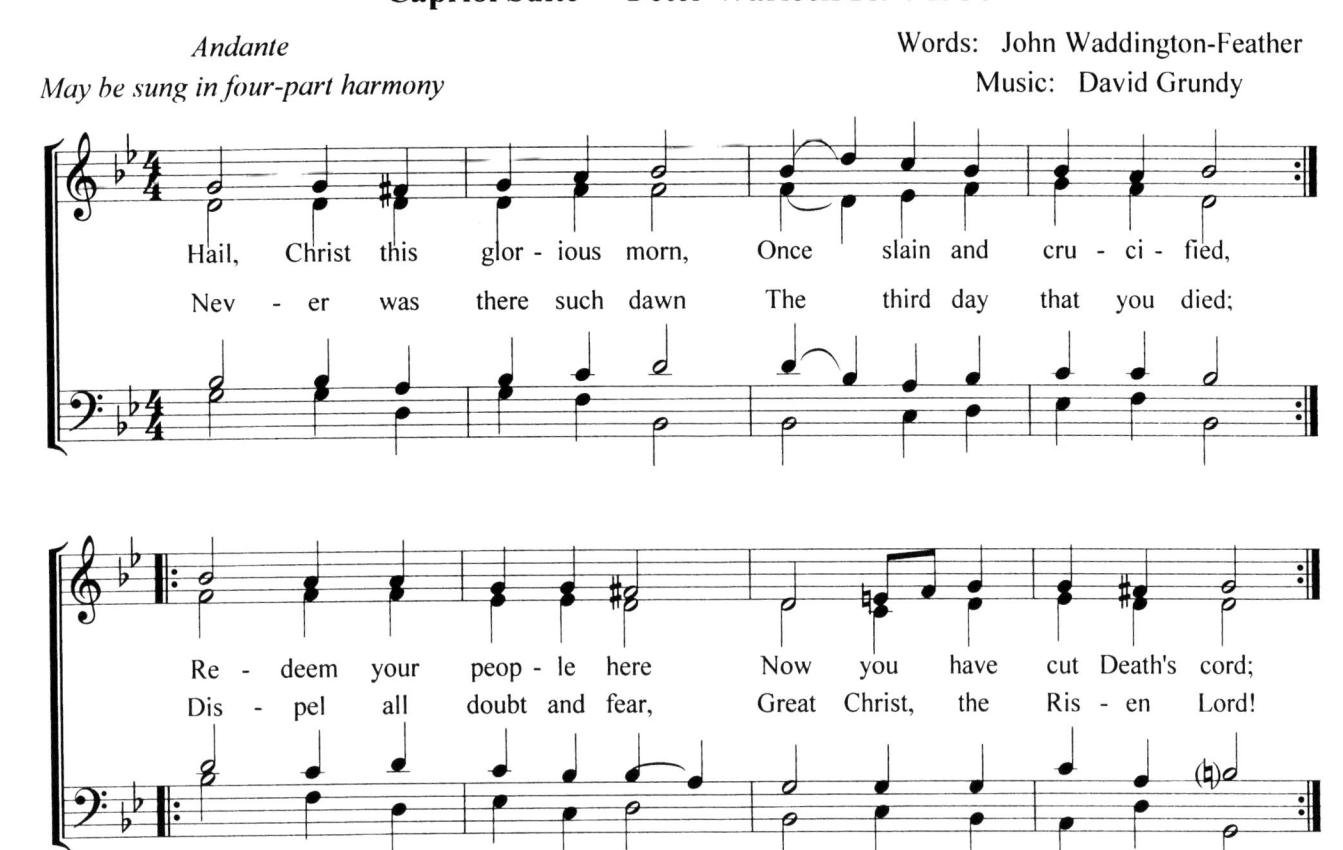

15

Andante

May be sung in four-part harmony

Words: John Waddington-Feather
Music: David Grundy

Hail, Christ this glor-ious morn, Once slain and cru-ci-fied,
Nev-er was there such dawn The third day that you died;
Re-deem your peop-le here Now you have cut Death's cord;
Dis-pel all doubt and fear, Great Christ, the Ris-en Lord!

2. All hail to you O Lord,
New risen from the dead;
All-conqu'ring, Lord supreme,
Our glorious King and Head.

3. Dread death, by God's Son slain,
All Evil overthrown,
You freed us from our sin,
Come, Jesus, claim your own!.

www.waddysweb.freeuk.com
Copyright words: John Waddington-Feather 2004
music: David Grundy 2004

Happy Those People
Entr'acte from "Rosamunde" SCHUBERT 1797-1828

Four-part harmony optional,
flowing tempo

Words: John Waddington-Feather
Music: arr. David Grundy

Hap - py those peop - le liv - ing in in the Lord,

Blessed are their spir - its nurt - ured by his Word. For in

Him they'll find peace in sil - ent dail - y prayer;

Repeat ad lib.

Heal - ing the mind and spir - it of each fret - ful care.

Instrumental interlude - top line melody, keyboard accompaniment.

Copyright words: John Waddington-Feather 2005
music: David Grundy 2005

16 *Happy those people (Contd (2)*

Resume singing here.

O send your peace up-on us, Lord, we pray

Holy Spirit - Communion Hymn
From Symphony No. 9 (Finale) - BEETHOVEN 1770-1827

17

Spiritedly
May be sung in four-part harmony

Words: John Waddington-Feather
Music: arr. David Grundy

1. Holy Spirit, we commend
Our lives and all we have to you;
Guide the gifts that God has given
In the way we know is true.

Bind us tightly in the family
Of the Christ who is the head;
Heal the differences dividing,
By the wine and by the bread.
Repeat the last four lines

2. By your blood and by your body
work your will among us, Lord;
Drawing us in full communion
To the power of your Word.

Till in oneness all men follow
Christ to God, the Three in One,
Father, Holy Spirit working
Through the teachings of the Son
Repeat the last four lines.

www.waddysweb.freeuk.com
Copyright Words: John Waddington-Feather 2004
Music: David Grundy 2004

18

How Beautiful This England
Vltava (from "My Country)
SMETANA 1824-84

Allegro comodo
To be sung in unison

Words: John Waddington-Feather
Music: arr. David Grundy

1. How beaut-i-ful this Eng-land, Lord, in con-cord with you, when land tilled, its wood-land crown and all earth stands true; and un-poll-ut-ed Eng-land is green, pleas-ant still, un-folds it-self thro' verd-ant vale and o'er roll-ing hill.

2. How beaut-i-ful its lakes and meres, its moors reach-ing high, such wild-ness of heath-ered heights which sweep to the sky; such beaut-y all a-round, Lord, we must hold it dear, cre-ate an-oth-er Ed-en and cher-ish it here.

www.waddysweb.freeuk.com
Copyright Words: John Waddington-Feather 2004
Music: David Grundy 2004

English Summer
19 From "Bohemia's Meadows and Forests" - SMETANA 1824-84

Slowish tempo, but flowing
Four-part harmony optional

Words: John Waddington-Feather
Music: arr. David Grundy

Id-yll-ic summer day — An Engl-ish mead-ow in hay, The balm-y air, all scent-filled, the sky-lark's const-ant song, spread far and wide, this sum-mer day.

God made this sum-mer day, The whole of heav-en at play, For here on earth, God shows us such liv-ing beau-ty and Splend-our on a glor-ious sum-mer day.

Give us the grace this day, To thank you, Lord, so we pray, For all the bless-ings God grants us day by day, such bount-y from a-bove, this sum-mer day.

Copyright words: John Waddington-Feather 2004
music: David Grundy 2004

WISDOM HYMN

20 **In all of our learning**

Academic Festival Overture - BRAHMS 1833-97

Boldly

May be sung in four-part harmony

Words: John Waddington-Feather
Music: arr. David Grundy

In all of our learning, good Lord, be our guide, Inspire us with your Spirit For ever at our side: That right and truth may triumph, Your word in us reside.

2. All wisdom is yours, Lord,
All justice and truth,
In righteous pathways lead us,
The way ahead be smooth,
That we may have your wisdom
In old age and in youth.

3. And give us the wisdom
To choose what is right
To help us build the Kingdom
Of everlasting light,
The world's dark night illumine,
And give all doubters sight.

Copyright Words: John Waddington-Feather 2005
Music: David Grundy 2005

PRAYER OF PENITENCE

21 The Earl of Salisbury's Pavane - WILLIAM BYRD c.1542-1623

Moderato

May be sung in four-part harmony

Words: John Waddiongton-Feather
Music: arr. David Grundy

Jes - u, good Lord, for - give us all our sins, And
Jes - u, sweet Lord, O cleanse us by your Blood.

our sins.
your Blood.

Tempt - er's guile O Lord
guard us from the Tempt - er's guile, O Lord our God. *(Organ)*

From all our wrongs de - liv - er us, Take from us our

guilt - Cleanse us com - plete - ly by your Blood.

Copyright Words: John Waddington-Feather 2004
Music: David Grundy 2004

Jesus, Lord (Hymn for Pentecost)
March of the Priests from "The Magic Flute" - MOZART

Andante con moto
May be sung in four-part harmony

Words: John Waddington-Feather
Music: arr. David Grundy

Jes - us, Lord, send down your Ho - ly Spi - rit, Give us the power to work and man - i - fest your ho - ly bid - ding; Fear - less to fol - low and heed - less of all dan - ger Yet eag - er to pro - claim your migh - ty words and acts of love.

Help us, Lord, to lis - ten to your teach - ing, Ev - er a - live to fol - low where your Spir - it, Lord, may lead us,

www.waddysweb.freeuk.com
Copyright words: John Waddington-Feather 2004
music: David Grundy 2004

Lead Us, Daily

23 "Romanza", from Horn Concerto No. 3, K.447 - MOZART 1756-91

Moderato
To be sung in unison

Words: John Waddington-Feather
Music: David Grundy

Optional instrumental part

Lead us, dail-y on our way, And with your Spir-it guide us; Keep at bay our dead-ly Foe, And in your lov-ing merc-y ev-er hide us; Strength-en us in times of weak-ness lest we fall; Keep our spir-its ev-er op-en to your call. Grac-ious Lord, stay close by our side, And through life's dark dis-tract-ions be our dail-y guide.

Repeat ad lib.

Copyright words: John Waddington-Feather 2004
music: David Grundy 2004

Hymn of Joy and Praise
Academic Festival Overture - BRAHMS 1833-97
"Gaudeamus Igitur"

Strongly
May be sung in four-part harmony

Words: John Waddington-Feather
Music: arr. David Grundy

1. Let us all re-joice in God, Praise to Him who made us.
Let our faith pro-claim our joy, here on earth and al-ways.
Bless-ings free-ly poured up-on us, Dail-y gifts from God a-bove us,
Des-pite all pain and grief, We're sur-round-ed by his love.

2. Let us gladly sing our praise
To our God most wonderful;
Let our hymns and anthems raise
Thanks to God most powerful;
Far beyond all words' expression
Offer music's jubilation;
Alleluia! Alleluia!
Your glory, Lord, we praise

Copyright Words: John Waddington-Feather 2005
Music: David Grundy 2005

25
Gavotte- Let Us Dance and Sing
From - "Holberg Suite" E. GRIEG 1843-1907

(With Optional Instrumental/Dance Episodes)

Words: John Waddington-Feather
Music: David Grundy

Let us dance and let us sing, Off-er-ing mus-ic glad-ly to God: Sing-ing, mov-ing in acc-ord, Danc-ing for joy, an off'-ring to the Lord.

Fine

Dance/Instrumental Episode 1

Let us dance and let us sing, Off-er-ing mus-ic glad-ly to God: Sing-ing, mov-ing in acc-ord, Danc-ing for joy, an off'-ring to the Lord.

Dance/Instrumental Episode 2

Copyright words: John Waddington-Feather 2005
music: David Grundy 2005

No. 25 Gavotte - Contd. (2)

Let us dance and let us sing, Off-er-ing mus-ic glad-ly to God: Sing-ing, mov-ing in acc-ord, Danc-ing for joy, an off'-ring to the Lord.

Dance/Instrumental Episode 3

1.

D.C.

Let us

Note: Instrumental interludes may be played on a keyboard.

A Prayer
Sonata Pathetique Op. 13 (2nd Mt) - BEETHOVEN 1770-1828

Words: John Waddington-Feather
Music: arr. David Grundy

Adagio

Lord God, Fath-er, give us your sweet grace And cleanse us from ev-il, Re-store us in your im-age.

Instrumental part

im-age.

Copyright Words: John Waddington-Feather 2004
Music: David Grundy 2004

LENTEN PSALM - A Choral Piece
Based on figured bass of Albinoni by Giazotto

Four-part harmony optional
Organ accompaniment ad lib.

Words: John Waddington-Feather
Music: David Grundy

Optional Organ Introduction when sung by a choir.

Lord God, our Redeemer, send down your mercy, Pardon our sins, grant us your grace, that we may rest in your peace. So may we, Lord, we may rest, may rest in peace. Amen. Amen.

Pardon our sins, grant us your grace, that we may rest in your peace, that we may rest, may rest in peace, peace. Amen. Amen.

Copyright Words: John Waddington-Feather 2004
Music: David Grundy 2004

Lord Jesus, Ever Constant
From Symphony No. 6 ("Pathetique") - 1st Mt.
TCHAIKOWSKY 1840-93

28

Solo or unison song, with organ accompaniment

Words: John Waddington-Feather
Music: arr. David Grundy

Lord Jesus, ever constant by my side, My life's companion and my heav'nly guide; Teach me the right way, Teach me, Lord, each day To follow you whatever may betide.

2. Lord Jesus, teach me daily pray aright,
For what is worthy always in your sight;
Not for myself, Lord,
But for your world, Lord,
Brought into your all-healing, glorious Light.

3. Make me a channel of your saving Grace,
That others see you, Jesus, face to face;
Boundless your great love,
Oh, such profound love,
God-sent to bring us to our heavenly place.

Copyright words: John Waddington-Feather 2004
music: David Grundy 2004

For Christ the King
A Choral Piece
From Overture - "Carnival Romain" - BERLIOZ 1803-69

Words: John Waddington-Feather
Music: arr. David Grundy

Slowish tempo

O Christ, the King, we praise your di-vine maj-est-y, We praise and ad-ore you with ful-ness of our mind and heart. *Fine*

For you, Christ Lord, our Mast-er and our Broth-er, you shower us with bless-ings with love ___ from your King-dom on high.

Ac-cept, Lord, all of our prais-es and thanks-giv-ing.

Copyright Words: John Waddington-Feather 2004
Music: David Grundy 2004

ONENESS

30 **A Solo Song, for High Voice with Piano or Organ Accompaniment**
"Aylesford Pieces" for Keyboard - HANDEL 1685-1759

Words: John Waddington-Feather
Music: arr. David Grundy

Con moto

Solo voice

O God our Father, kindle our spirit, help us rejoice, delight in your living world; The earth that feeds us and all that live in it stars up above, seas in lowest deep, You are revealed.

O God our Father, give us compassion, help us to love and respect all here on earth; You breathe your Spirit on all you fashion, from man's image to lowest cell, All in you, One.

[v.2]

Copyright words: John Waddington-Feather 2005
music: David Grundy 2005

31 — O Jesus, My Saviour (Healing)
Symphony No. 1 (Finale) BRAHMS 1833-97

Boldly
May be sung in four-part harmony

Words: John Waddington-Feather
Music: arr. David Grundy

1. O, Jesus, my Saviour, my Master and my Lord,
O, Jesus my Saviour, the Guardian of my being.
You lead me through all times of stress,
through times when faith seems lost;
Lord, bring us back to you again,
to bathe in your glory.

2. O, Jesus, my Saviour, my Comforter and Help,
O, Jesus, God's glory, the light of every nation.
Take me and use me in your service
now and evermore,
Lord Jesus, you are the one who brings us
life everlasting.

www.waddysweb.freeuk.com
Copyright Words: John Waddington-Feather 2004
Music: David Grundy 2004

Springtime Hymn
32 From Quintet for Piano and Wind, K.452 - MOZART 1756-91

To be sung in a sprightly fashion, in unison

Words: John Waddington-Feather
Music: arr. David Grundy

O, re - joice in God's great good - ness and be thank - ful for his bount - y. In this spring - time's glor - ious ful - ness As new life bursts from the ground.

O, re - joice our Lord is ris - en, come a - live to save his peop - le, New re - leased from three - day pris - on, reign - ing here for ev - er more.

O, re - joice, re - joice, you Christ - ians In your Fath - er God this spring - time; Oh, re - joice, re - joice you Christ - ians In your Lord who conqu - ered death.

Copyright words: John Waddington-Feather 2004
music: David Grundy 2004

Wedding Song
From the opera "Oberon", by C.M. von Weber 1786-1826

A solo song, with organ accompaniment

Words: John Waddington-Feather
Music: arr. David Grundy

1. O, happy day! Most blessed of morns! Together in wedlock a happy future dawns, And as time rolls out its tale still un-told, May you grow closer still as years all un-fold.

2. Two now as one, both partners for life, to help each other in good times and in strife, To comfort, sustain, in sickness in health, Uphold your vows in poverty and in wealth.

3. Christ light your way and God bless your bond, Fruitful your love be both here and beyond; May you take abroad Christ's love to the world, Your marriage his light, his banner bright unfurled.

www.waddysweb.freeuk.com
Copyright words: John Waddington-Feather 2004
music: David Grundy 2004

Trinity Hymn

34   **MENDELSSOHN - Finale of "Scottish Symphony"**

2 beats to the bar
May be sung in four-part harmony

Words: John Waddngton-Feather
Music: arr. David Grundy

1. One God, one Christ, one Holy Spirit be o'er us,
 guide us on our way, your threefold banner before us,
 to fit us for life, O heavenly Father, restore us.

2. Creator God, who made the earth and the heavens,
 Oh, shine down your light, that we may be forgiven,
 renewed in your Son, and lead us to your haven.

3. Our Saviour Christ, who came to earth to save us,
 to preach the good news, that sin no longer enslaves us,
 and rose from the dead, to show that God forgave us.

4. Spirit divine, on earth to comfort and guide us,
 O, shine forth your light and may your counsel precede us,
 with your holy truth, O nourish us and feed us.

Feather Books
www.waddysweb.freeuk.com
Copyright Words: John Waddington-Feather 2004
Music: David Grundy 2004

CHRIST'S PRESENCE
Our Saviour Is Beside Us
"The Limetree" - SCHUBERT 1797-1828

35

Slow tempo
Four-part harmony optional

Words: John Waddington-Feather
Music: arr. David Grundy

1. Our Saviour is beside us in happiness and pain. He shares our mortal being, in sunshine and in rain. He knows the world's condition, Its conflicts and its sin; O, open up your hearts to him And let your Saviour in.

2. Our Saviour died at Calv'ry
To make his people whole;
To wash away each blemish,
Restore the stricken soul.
He knows our faults and failings here,
For He was once a man;
And tempted like all people here,
But died and rose again.

3. And now He lives in Spirit
To lift us when we're down;
When Satan works upon us
To claim us as his own.
But we are Christ's dear children,
He's here in times of need;
And when by sickness prisoned
By Jesus we are freed.

Copyright words: John Waddington-Feather 2005
music: David Grundy 2005

The Power of Prayer
From "The Emperor" Piano Concerto (2nd Mt.)
BEETHOVEN 1770-1828

36

May be sung in four-part harmony
Quite slowly

Words: John Waddington-Feather
Music: arr. David Grundy

1. Peace comes in - to the soul, Heal - ing to make it whole; Sil - ent, deep - est prayer Dis - pers - es fret - ful care, Each hour by hour, Day by day, When to God we do kneel to pray. When to God we do kneel and pray.

2. Prayer eas - es dail - y stress, Calms us through push and press; Still - ing troub - led minds, Till sweet - est peace we find; Rest - or - ing faith, Bring - ing souls Back to Jes - sus to make us whole. Back to Jes - us to make us whole.

Copyright Words: John Waddington-Feather 2004
Music: David Grundy 2004

HYMN OF PRAISE
From the opera "The Pearl Fishers", by BIZET 1838-75

37

Four-part harmony optional
Organ accompaniment

Words: John Waddington-Feather
Music: arr. David Grundy

1. Praise our God, our Lord Creator,
   Praise the Lord with all your might;
   Praise our God, the one most holy,
   From lowest deeps to heaven's height.
   Praise him all you sons of glory,
   Day by day and night by night;

   Praise him, daughters, of the true God,
   Precious all within his sight.

   (Repeat last two lines)

2. Praise the Lord with joy, thanksgiving,
   Praise the Lord with music's sound;
   Praise the Lord your sweet chords ringing,
   Let your instruments resound;
   Let the mighty organ thunder
   Shake the earth from bound to bound,

   Raising hymns to highest heaven,
   Echo and re-echo round,

Copyright Words: John Waddington-Feather 2004
Music: David Grundy 2004

Sabbath Hymn
Praise We Our Lord This Day
Piano Sonata in A, D. 959 (Finale)　　SCHUBERT 1797-1828

38

Allegretto

Four-part harmony optional

Words: John Waddington-Feather
Music: arr. David Grundy

Praise we our Lord this day, Praise him for its glor - y.
We thank Him for our faith, And the Bib - le stor - y.
Praise, praise, praise our Lord! Com - mune in the wine and bread.
Op - en wide your hearts, By our Lord we all are fed.

Give thanks to God this day And its Sab - bath dawn - ing;
Thank Him for fell - ow ship Here with Him this morn - ing;
Shared with one and all, And with Jes - us Christ our Lord,
Liv - ing al - ways near us, through each day of our lives.

Copyright words: John Waddington-Feather 2005
music: David Grundy 2005

Save us, O Christ
39   Symphony No. 2 (Second Mt.) BEETHOVEN 1770-1827
A Hymn for Mental Health

Four-part harmony optional,
organ accompaniment ad lib. when sung by a choir.
Slow but flowing tempo

Words: John Waddington-Feather
Music: arr. David Grundy

1. Save us O Christ, from sin's ev-il power, that we may live life as peo-ple of God; free from ev'ry ad-dict-ion, from the world's sad aff-lict-ion, to foll-ow you on-ly and live with-in your grace; to foll-ow you, Jes-us, till we meet face to face.

2. Near us are you, when we are de-pressed, O lift us O Christ, from depths of des-pair; chang-ing bleak des-per-a-tion to new-found jub-il-at-ion, and ban-ish all dark-ness a-way by your love, that leads us, Lord Jes-us, un-to our home a-bove.

Words Copyright: John Waddington-Feather 2004
Music Copyright: David Grundy 2004

Shepherdman
"New World" Symphony (2nd Mt.) - DVORAK 1841-1904

Words: John Waddington-Feather
Music: arr. David Grundy

Largo

Organ Intro.

1. Shepherdman, Shepherdman, lead your flock safe home,
safe with you, Jesus Lord, never more to roam;
Shepherdman, lead your flock to its final fold,
safe from harm, close with youj, heaven to behold

2. Shepherdman, Shephardman, from the sad world's care,
lead us from barren land to your pastures fair;
take us Lord, help and guide, through death's darkling vale
forward to heaven's home and our God reveal.

This may be sung as a solo, with either organ or choral (humming) accompaniment

www.waddysweb.freeuk.com
Copyright words: John Waddington-Feather 2004
music: David Grundy 2004

41
Sing Aloud! (a happy-clappy hymn)
Scottish Folktune - "Kelvingrove"

Briskly
To be sung in unison

Words: John Waddington-Feather
Music: arr. David Grundy

1. Sing a-loud if you're happy and rejoice, rejoice! Lift your praises to heaven with full heart and voice; To our God give your praise and high your voices raise, Till the earth resounds with a gladsome noise.

2. Clap your hands if you're happy, Show the world your joy; Give thanks for the blessings we all enjoy; Clap your hands, praise the Lord, Who gave to us the Word, Showed the way to heav'n and th'angelic host.

Copyright words: John Waddington-Feather 2004
music: David Grundy 2004

Creation Praise Hymn
42 From Symphony No 3 ("Eroica") Finale BEETHOVEN

To be sung in unison.
Brisk tempo

Words: John Waddington-Feather
Music: arr. David Grundy

1. Sing high, sing low, sing praise to God! Sing all you folk, give praise to God on high! All men and wom-en here be-low Give God, our God, your praise! Sing all the world to our God on high!

2. Sing high, sing low, give praise to God! Sing ev'ry creat-ure made by Him be-low; You swirl-ing seas and rest-less waves, O thund-er out your praise! Sing all the world, to our God on high!

3. Sing high, sing low, you hills to God! Sing ev'ry moun-tain soar-ing to the sky! You roll-ing rang-es, loft-y peaks, O trump-et forth your praise! Sing all the world to our God on high!

4. Sing high, sing low, you stars to God! Sing con-stell-a-tions, dwell-ing there on high! You count-less plan-ets out in space, O sound your sil-ent praise! Sing, all cre-a-tion, to God on high!

Copyright words: John Waddington-Feather 2004
music: David Grundy 2004

Sing and Dance

43   **Air "Harmonious Blacksmith" - G.F. HANDEL 1685-1759**

Moderato
May be sung in four-part harmony

Words: John Waddington-Feather
Music: arr. David Grundy

1. Sing, O sing O sing with Jesus, Sing to God with all your heart! Sing you high and sing you low, O sing to God with all your might! Fill the world with joy and gladness, Happiness to heaven's height!
2. Dance, O dance, O dance with Jesus, Lift your limbs and tap your feet! Dance, O dance, O dance with Jesus, Make your dancing trim and neat, Dance, O dance, O dance with Jesus, Make your dancing trim and neat.
3. Swing to left and swing to right, O gladden hearts with ev'ry move! Leap with rhythm, in time with 'em, Glory in your father's love! Leap with rhythm, in time with 'em, Glory in your father's love!

www.waddysweb.freeuk.com
Copyright words: John Waddington-Feather 2005
music: David Grundy 2005

Easter Song

From Symphony No. 5 (2nd Movement)
Antonin Dvorak (1841-1904)

Words: John Waddington-Feather
Music: arr. David Grundy

Andante con moto

1. That Passion-tide, our Lord lay buried inside the stone cold tomb; and weeping, his disciples hurried to hide, frightened, anxious, in that barred-fast upper room
2. When Mary found that he had vanished, as she returned at dawn; She stood and wept and sadly languished, so weary, she turned and saw the gard'ner all forlorn.
3. She asked him where his men had laid him, since stark the tomb was bare; "O, Mary," she turned round and saw him, "Rabboni!" she saw him, our Lord Jesus, standing there.
4. Then Mary sped back to the others, still hid in upper room; exclaiming, "Sisters and brothers, he's risen! for ever from that dread and silent tomb."

Copyright words: John Waddington-Feather 2004
music: David Grundy 2004

MORNING HYMN
Symphony No. 88 - HAYDN 1732-1809

45

Con moto
May be sung in unison

Words: John Waddington-Feather
Music: arr. David Grundy

The small notes are part of Haydn's melody

The morn-ing has brok-en, the sweet sun is beam-ing its life-giv-ing rays up-on the fair earth, its light and its sweet-ness in ful-ness un-furled; then let us, this Sab-bath, give praise to the Fath-er, who sends count-less bless-ings up-on the whole world.

2, This morning, O Father, together we gather
to worship and glorify your Name,
to offer our prayers and our sins to confess,
that clean in our spirit, with joy and thangsgiving,
the whole week before us your Name we bless.

www.waddysweb.freeuk.com
Copyright Words: John Waddington-Feather 2004
Words: David Grundy 2004

There in the morning
From "Zemir et Azore" - GRETRY 1741-1813

46

Andante
To be sung in unison

Words: John Waddington-Feather
Music: arr. David Grundy

v.4 sacr - i - fice.

1. There in the morning, there in the evening,
Saviour Jesus, ever near;
here at our birthing, there at our ending,
sweet Lord, be ever near us.

2. Jesus, our Saviour, Comforter, Brother.
guide, we pray, throughout our life;
guard us and guide us through the world's turmoil
through all its endless strivings.

3. Teach us, good Master, more to be like you,
in all our doings with each one;
kindly and loving to all our neighbours,
treat all as sisters, brothers.

4. Give us the will to be forgiving,
as you forgave, Lord, paying the price;
building your Kingdom here by your teaching,
and by your sacrifice.

5. There in the morning, there in the evening,
Saviour Jesus, ever near;
here at our birthing, there at our ending,
sweet Lord, be ever near us.

www.waddysweb.freeuk.com
Copyright words: John Waddington-Feather 2004
music: David Grundy 2004

A National Song
This Pleasant Land
Concerto No. 1 (2nd Mt.) MAX BRUCH 1838-1920

Solo or unison song, with organ accompaniment — Words: John Waddington-Feather
A slow, but flowing tempo — Music: arr. David Grundy

Organ

1. This pleas-ant land of ours, and O so beaut-i-ful to see! It is so rich-ly blessed, a land that's bount-i-ful, an is-land home That's bount-i-ful and free.

2. This gent-le land of ours, the dear-est jew-el of the sea! Hav-en for many a race, Which sought their ref-uge here from tyr-an-ny, A land that's safe and free.

3. May God bless Eng-land still and help us rule it stead-fast-ly. May truth and peace a-bound With-in a just and fair and hap-py land, That lives in harm-on-y.

Copyright words: John Waddington-Feather 2005
music: David Grundy 2005

Harvest Hymn
After the "St. Anthony Chorale"
Michael Haydn (1737-1806)

Four-part harmony optional
Organ accompaniment ad lib. when sung by a choir.

Word: John Waddington-Feather
Music: arr. David Grundy

Moderate tempo

Wel-come in the harv-est with all joy and thanks-giv-ing. Thank God for our farm-ing work-ers, for their means of liv-ing; Fields are shorn and barns are full, and burst-ing are the sil-os high, Ploughed al-read-y wheat-en fields, while fall-ow oth-ers lie; Thanks to God the Giv-er, Un-i-vers-al Fath-er.

Give thanks for our fish-ers trawl-ing, through the oc-eans striv-ing Dang'-rous are their lab-ours for us, through the deep seas driv-ing.

Copyright Words: John Waddington-Feather 2004
Music: David Grundy 2004

Advent Hymn
49 **Pilgrims' March from "Italian" Symphony MENDELSSOHN 1809-47**

To be sung in a stately manner
Four-part harmony optional

Words: John Waddington-Feather
Music: arr. David Grundy

Optional Introduction

1. When God came down to earth from heaven
the angels sang their songs of praise,
the shepherds left their flocks by night
to worship Christ the King;
and Wise Men did their homage pay
and brought great gifts of countless price
when God the Lord came down to earth
and showed Himself as man

2. But when He comes the second time,
He'll sit on His great Judgement Throne
and bring all people to His rule
to winnow out the chaff.
He'll separate the good and bad
and leave the evil to their lot,
but draw his people to Himself
to dwell with Him in heaven.

Copyright Words: John Waddington-Feather 2004
Music: David Grundy 2004

Discipleship

50   **Symphony No. 7 (2nd Movement) - DVORAK 1841-1904**

Slowish tempo
May be sung in four-part harmony

Words: John Waddington-Feather
Music: David Grundy

When Saint Pet-er heard the call He left his nets by Gal-i-lee Lake: Saint And-rew al-so was drawn to Christ And foll-owed him in Pet-er's wake.

2. James and John, old Zebedee's sons,
They heard our Lord, left nets unfurled;
Those first disciples listened to Christ,
And took his teaching to the world.

3. Others, too, obeyed Christ's call
And followed him right to the end;
They saw him raised up high on a cross,
Come back to life and then ascend

4. Back to God to reign above,
Yet left his Church on earth below,
With twelve apostles whom Jesus chose
As channels for his grace to flow.

5. We today must heed his call
And follow where the Lord may lead,
Through time and space, spread God's holy Word
And help our Lord his flock to feed.

www.waddysweb.freeuk.com
Copyright words: John Waddington-Feather 2004
music: David Grundy 2004